HOW SAFE
ARE WE?

HOW SAFE ARE WE?

Homeland Security Since 9/11

JANET NAPOLITANO

with KAREN BRESLAU

PUBLICAFFAIRS
New York

PublicAffairs
Hachette Book Group
1290 Avenue of the Americas, New York, NY 10104
www.publicaffairsbooks.com
@Public_Affairs

Printed in the United States of America

First Edition: March 2019

Published by PublicAffairs, an imprint of Perseus Books, LLC, a subsidiary of Hachette Book Group, Inc. The PublicAffairs name and logo is a trademark of the Hachette Book Group.

The Hachette Speakers Bureau provides a wide range of authors for speaking events. To find out more, go to www.hachettespeakersbureau.com or call (866) 376-6591.

The publisher is not responsible for websites (or their content) that are not owned by the publisher.

Print book interior design by Amnet Systems.

Library of Congress Cataloging-in-Publication Data

Names: Napolitano, Janet, author. | Breslau, Karen, author.
Title: How safe are we? : homeland security since 9/11 / Janet Napolitano
   with Karen Breslau.
Description: First edition. | New York : PublicAffairs, [2019] | Includes
   index.
Identifiers: LCCN 2018044613 (print) | LCCN 2018054195 (ebook) | ISBN
   9781541762213 (ebook) | ISBN 9781541762220 (hardcover)
Subjects: LCSH: Napolitano, Janet. | United States. Department of Homeland
   Security. | National security—United States. | Internal security—United
   States. | Terrorism—United States—Prevention. | United States—Politics
   and government—1989-
Classification: LCC HV6432.4 (ebook) | LCC HV6432.4 .N36 2019 (print) | DDC
   363.34092 [B]—dc23
LC record available at https://lccn.loc.gov/2018044613

ISBNs: 978-1-5417-6222-0 (hardcover); 978-1-5417-6221-3 (ebook)
LSC-C

10   9   8   7   6   5   4   3   2   1

For my family and for my friends, who have often acted as a supplemental family. (You know who you are.) For all the colleagues I have had the privilege of working with during my years in public service. It has been my honor to serve alongside you. And finally, for the American people, whose spirit never ceases to amaze and inspire me.

CONTENTS

INTRODUCTION

Like most Americans of a certain age, I remember exactly where I was and what I was doing when our country was attacked on the morning of September 11, 2001. It was shortly before 7:00 a.m. in Phoenix, Arizona, and I was home getting ready for work when I heard on NPR that a plane had flown into one of the World Trade Center towers. The cause was being described as a possible air traffic control problem. A few minutes later, as I was drying my hair, I heard the announcement that stopped me cold—that the second tower had been hit. I knew then, along with the rest of America, that this wasn't an accident.

I was the attorney general of Arizona at that time, and the moment I heard that the second tower had been hit, I dropped my hair dryer and went into crisis mode. I called my chief of staff to activate our team and run through our plan should there be an attack on Arizona. A few minutes later, I got a call from Governor Jane Dee Hull, asking whether she had the legal authority to scramble National Guard jets to protect the state's Palo Verde Nuclear Generating Station, the largest power plant in the nation. I took a beat. It's in my nature to plan for everything, to prepare for every eventuality, but there was no plan for this. I had to make a call. I told the governor that without authorization from the Pentagon, she could not activate the Guard, since it was both a federal and a state asset. By this point, we'd learned that the Pentagon had also been hit by a commercial airliner and was in flames. There would be no answer from Washington that day.

As a high-level state government official, the near silence from the federal government was eerie. In the chaotic first hours after the attacks, President George W. Bush was aboard Air Force One, flanked by F-16s, as he was flown from one military base to another, unable to communicate reliably with his cabinet, leaders of Congress, or the American people. With the president out of the public eye for the moment, New York City mayor Rudolph Giuliani emerged for many as the face and voice of the government response on that first day and the days that followed. In that task, he performed admirably.

Everyone was scrambling to understand what was happening, including cabinet secretaries, governors, mayors, police chiefs, first responders, the media, and, of course, the American public. People were terrified, wondering what could happen next and where to get reliable and actionable information. It wasn't until I got home late that night and watched people jumping from the burning towers on television that the impact of the day hit me. As I numbly watched endless video loops of office workers plunging to the ground to avoid being consumed by flames, I could only think about what horrors they must have been faced with to make the decision to jump. Those images remain seared in my memory to this day, as they do for many of us.

We will soon observe the twentieth anniversary of the Tuesday that transformed our nation so profoundly that it is known most commonly by its date: 9/11 (like December 7, 1941, Pearl Harbor, or November 22, 1963, the assassination of President John F. Kennedy). The 9/11 attacks changed the way we fly, protect our borders, investigate crime, and gather government information. They changed the way we organize the federal government itself, the economy, and even the way we watch the news on television. (The nonstop news ticker screen crawl was born to handle the torrent of information that day.) The 9/11 attacks shook the American psyche too, in ways that continue to reverberate. It had been nearly sixty years since the Japanese bombed Pearl Harbor, and for the first time in the lives of most Americans, we had to struggle with the realization that we were no longer safe from attack by a foreign entity within the borders of the United States. This altered our expectations of what our government can and cannot do for us. It affected our politics; it challenged our conception of ourselves as the world's most open society.

It's been nearly two decades since 9/11, and I believe it's time to take stock of those changes, to identify which policies that were put in place back then still work and which ones need to be fixed. In those early days after the attacks, decisions were made and laws were passed that were the result of fear, lack of information, and often a sincere desire to ensure that kind of attack would never happen again. It's time to look at those decisions in light of the country we are today and to address the new threats that have arisen in the nearly two decades since the attacks.

Think of this book as an American report card. What has worked and what has not? What are the social, political, and economic costs of that progress? Where are our biggest vulnerabilities today, and how do we repair them? What are the risks we must accept if we are to remain a free and open society? What should government do for us, and what must each of us do for ourselves and our neighbors in the event of emergency? Most importantly, are we safer and more resilient today than we were on September 11, 2001?

One of the biggest changes resulting from 9/11 was the creation of the Department of Homeland Security in early 2003. The job of the department is broad: to protect the nation's air, land, and sea borders and to manage our immigration system and oversee the federal government's resources for responding to disasters of all types. Unlike the Department of Defense, which was created after World War II, the Department of Homeland Security (DHS) is primarily a civilian agency. It has domestic law-enforcement and intelligence-gathering functions, in addition to its global responsibilities. And it is enormous. DHS is the third-largest agency in the federal government, behind the Departments of Defense and Veterans Affairs, with 240,000 employees.

I was the third secretary of homeland security, after Tom Ridge and Michael Chertoff, and the first to be appointed by President Barack Obama. I came to the cabinet in 2009, leaving as governor of Arizona during my second term and following my career in law enforcement, including stints as Arizona's attorney general and as US Attorney for the District of Arizona. I left the administration late in 2013 to become president of the University of California, proud of the considerable progress we'd made at DHS in a relatively short time to improve border security, transportation security, and the government's abilities to respond to emergencies of all types.

The 9/11 attacks were as close to a decapitating attack on the United States government as we have seen, and they laid bare the shortcomings of our government to protect us in the age of terror. Over the past fifteen years, through Republican and Democratic administrations alike, we have come a long way to ensure that the government cannot be immobilized again. The Department of Homeland Security has developed playbooks, constantly updated, for nearly every catastrophe and scenario imaginable. Working with the Departments of Defense and Justice, the intelligence agencies, the Congress, our allies, and thousands of local governments, law-enforcement partners, and first responders, we have gotten much better at identifying and guarding against many threats as they emerge. We are more strategic and more aggressive as a result of these efforts and have made Americans safer, more prepared, and more resilient in the face of many disasters than they were before 9/11.

We did a lot, both seen and unseen, to increase airport security while giving millions of qualified US travelers TSA Precheck status, expediting their passage through our airports. I must admit, though, that I am frustrated we did not make enough progress during the Obama administration on improving the capabilities of the screening process so that people can leave their shoes on and carry liquids on their flights easily. Faced with limited resources, technological limitations, and competing security priorities, we had to focus first on safety, even when that meant continued inconvenience for the traveling public.

We did make significant advances in other aspects of border security. Based on the science of risk analysis, we designed effective systems to screen and stop dangerous passengers, vehicles, vessels, and cargo from entering the United States. We improved intelligence sharing, both within the US government and among our allies, to detect threats to the United States farther from our borders and to intercept those who would do harm before they make it to US soil, airspace, or maritime borders. We pushed illegal crossings along our border with Mexico to a forty-year low and improved border security with advanced technology to support our expanded force of US Border Patrol agents.

We remade the Federal Emergency Management Agency (FEMA) into one of the most efficient and effective agencies of the federal government. I can say this confidently because it was put to the test in national and global emergencies, including the Deepwater Horizon oil spill in the Gulf of Mexico in 2010, delivering US aid to Haiti following its devastation by an earthquake in 2010, and Hurricane Sandy along the East Coast in 2012, among many other extreme weather events.

We integrated two dozen component agencies, thrown together amid the trauma following 9/11 into a single, integrated Department of Homeland Security with a shared mission to defend the American homeland and help the American people become more resilient.

Yet we still face enormous threats. They are multiplying, more diffuse and more virulent than ever, and our efforts to manage these new dangers reveal mixed results. The federal government has not kept up with the pace and sophistication of cyberattacks against our critical infrastructure—indeed, against our democracy itself—led by such adversaries as Russia, North Korea, and our great power rival, China, as well as those by nonstate actors, whose motives are sometimes less clear. The threats from terrorism have evolved as well since 9/11—from centralized, stateless organizations, such as al-Qaeda under the leadership of Osama bin Laden, to decentralized, leaderless terror networks that inspire adherents all over the world on the internet and exhort them to strike in place. We see the rise of right-wing violence as well and of mass casualty events, including shootings in schools and other public venues, that appear prompted by no political ideology at all. The surge in natural disasters linked to climate change threatens more Americans than all other causes rolled together.

Americans in general are straight-talking, fact-based problem solvers. So let's embrace our nature. Let's face these facts, talk openly about them, and come up with solutions. One of the most important things we all must understand better are the ways in which technology has changed and is changing the threat landscape since September 11, 2001. On that day, there were no smartphones, no Facebook, no Twitter, and no apps. Google was only three years old. Texting was possible but was such a pain on a flip phone that most people didn't bother.

Osama bin Laden was adept at the technology of his day, recording threats on videotape cassettes that were smuggled from his hideout in the caves between Afghanistan and Pakistan by couriers and then mailed or delivered to Arab-language satellite networks. Intelligence analysts pored over the striations in the cave wall behind bin Laden, the vegetation in the background, or the label on his plastic water bottle, anything that could help to pinpoint the location and time of the recording. American television anchors explained that the tapes were authenticated, frowning their disapproval and playing short clips with subtitles while explaining that the portions selected for airtime were deemed not to pose a danger to the public.

Today, bin Laden is long dead, killed by a US Navy SEAL team in 2011. His surviving lieutenants are long in the tooth. Al-Qaeda has metastasized and rebranded itself into ISIS, now dispersed in locations throughout the Middle East, Europe, Asia, Africa, and North America. Its tactics against civilians are even more savage than those used on 9/11. The rise of social media networks and dark web browsers allow lone wolves to find with relative ease the inspiration and DIY tools to commit mass murder without crossing an international border. Traditional surveillance and law-enforcement tools are stretched to intercept these plots in time.

As of this writing, we are still struggling to comprehend the ways in which Russia used technology to compromise our 2016 presidential election and seeking stronger methods to deter future intrusions into our electoral systems. If election tampering by a foreign power isn't a threat to the homeland, I don't know what is. It remains to be seen how deceptive ads on Facebook and other social media platforms, the infiltration of individual state voting systems, and the hacking of email accounts associated with Hillary Clinton and her aides influenced the election—or whether these factors did or did not change the outcome. Official investigations into what happened in 2016 are backward-looking and mired in partisan battles. We are still struggling with the most consequential challenge: how to prevent it from happening again. Technology evolves faster all the time, and the US government, along with the state governments that manage elections, scramble to keep pace. We need clarity about who leads the federal government response to cyberattacks and what role the private sector should play. We need to better coordinate our defenses going forward—and present a united front to any adversary who threatens the infrastructure of American democracy.

Some vulnerabilities are more perceived than real, yet these are no less vexing to the American people. In this category, I include the persistent political hysteria over the security of the US border with Mexico. Most Americans have a fragile understanding of this vast region of the country, and this makes it ripe for demagoguery. In 2018, we saw the appalling spectacle of migrant children being separated from their parents after they were detained for crossing illegally into the United States, under a misguided "zero tolerance" policy. Of course our country needs secure borders, but that's where the demagoguery starts. Americans are told they have to choose between an "open" border, over which undocumented migrants pour "by the millions" and "infest" the country, or a "big beautiful" wall. This is a false choice. The most heavily trafficked land border in the world cannot be sealed like a Ziploc bag. We can have a secure border and the rule of law, as reasonable Democrats and Republicans agree. It is not beyond us to come up with policies that facilitate the legal flows of people and commerce vital to our economy and at the same time deter illegal traffic using smart technology and strategic law enforcement.

Despite tremendous advances in reducing illegal flows of people and contraband over the southern border during the Obama administration, I don't think we communicated as effectively as we could have with the American people about our progress. We could not break through with the facts about the connection between that difficult mission of securing the border and the need for comprehensive immigration reform to fix our broken system. If your boat is leaking, you do not choose between bailing water and repairing the hole. You do one and then the other. Immigration reform means three things: first, continuing to secure the southern border in a way consistent with our laws and values and the best technology; second, designing a visa system that is fair and consistent with dynamic US labor needs and international humanitarian obligations; and third, building a functional immigration system that puts the eleven million undocumented people in the United States on a path to legal status. Only if we do all three will we prevent such a backlog from developing again.

Nearly twenty years after 9/11, we are witnessing homeland security malpractice: an administration that aggressively refuses to recognize threats that are real and certain, coupled with an equally aggressive effort to divert public attention and government resources toward issues that are less lethal, but more potent politically. A migrant caravan from Central America is easier to see on television than is climate change, or an adversary's digital incursions into our elections and other critical infrastructure, but that doesn't make it a greater danger to our way of life. None of this lessens the terror Americans inflict on other Americans in our public spaces through mass gun violence.

In our fractious political and social climate today, it is worth thinking back to the aftermath of 9/11 in another way. I don't miss the emotional pain or the fear of that time. What I do miss is our sense of togetherness—the belief that we were bound by ideals and a commitment to justice to hold each other up through the darkness, no matter our politics, our religion, or our ethnic origins. The United States had taken a terrible blow, but the fabric of our society was strong. Recall the members of Congress singing the national anthem on the steps of the Capitol, people holding candles on their front porches that night and dropping off baked goods at their local fire stations, the lines at blood banks around the country from people desperate to give something to save a life—even though the emergency rooms in Manhattan were nearly empty because so few of the victims of the attacks even survived. I remember the crowds lining the West Side Highway, cheering the ironworkers who had driven to New York City from across the country to untangle the twisted remnants of the Twin Towers, in case there was a life to be saved or remains to recover with dignity. The government didn't ask them to come. They loaded their tools, got in their trucks, and drove.

We were perhaps never more American than we were on that day and in the days and months that followed. Young and not-so-young Americans flocked to military service, the foreign service, the intelligence services, and to other forms of public service. We didn't talk about the "deep state"; we talked about our deep reverence for our state, our nation, and our place in the world. And the United States was not alone; the community of nations joined with us in our grief and horror. For the first time since its founding in 1949, NATO invoked Article 5, the alliance's mutual defense clause, declaring an attack on one is an attack on all. The French daily *Le Monde* headline "Nous sommes tous américains" (We are all Americans) resonated throughout the world. Parisians stood in front of Notre Dame singing "The Star Spangled Banner." In Great Britain, Queen Elizabeth II authorized the US national anthem to be played during the changing of the guard at Buckingham Palace, and traffic came to a halt. In Germany, two hundred thousand people marched through the streets of Berlin in solidarity. Even adversaries responded. In Iran, thousands stood for a moment of silence before a soccer match. North Korea sent condolences.

Everything changed on 9/11, and some of the good things that came out of that terrible time have since faded along with the bad. We can and we must restore our sense of common purpose. In this book, I'll take you through my time at the DHS and what I experienced more broadly during decades of public service. If you are looking for dirt, buy a book on gardening. At a time when it is fashionable to malign the motives and qualifications of people who choose to work in government, it is worth reminding ourselves that our democracy depends on citizens willing to lend their talents and ideas, taking on huge responsibilities, and not for a giant paycheck. It is my hope that my story might inspire more good people to find that common purpose once again and step up to serve.

PART I

THE MISSION

CHAPTER 1

What Have I Done?

The dolly was my first clue. From my office on the ninth floor of the Arizona State Capitol, I watched as an aide wheeled it toward me, piled high with bulging white binders in precarious stacks. It was mid-December, and in only a few weeks, I would trade the job I loved as governor of Arizona to become US secretary of homeland security, only the third in our nation's history. My predecessor, Michael Chertoff, wanted to make sure I had everything I needed to be prepared for running the newest, most sprawling, and, as yet, least understood agency of the federal government. These transition binders contained playbooks, memos, and intelligence, all aimed at helping me deal with everything in the Homeland Security portfolio, from terrorists to tornadoes, plagues and pandemics, planes, trains, and automobiles, to immigration and border security, cyberweapons, an attack on the power grid or water system, and biological and chemical warfare and nuclear dirty bombs.

Michael Chertoff had been President George W. Bush's secretary of homeland security, a capable and thoughtful federal prosecutor and judge by training, and he did everything he could to ensure a smooth transition. Each of the many binders opened with a memorandum describing the current state of a particular issue, the initiatives underway, the related budget framework, the number of employees working on it, pending decisions that would carry into President Obama's term, and a timeline for decisions that had to be made. The clocks on many of these decisions were already ticking, which required a high-speed baton pass from the Bush administration to President Obama's. I'm the kind of person who likes organized timelines and clear goals, and especially since I was still wrapping up my responsibilities as governor, I felt a deep sense of urgency. People's lives were at stake with most of these decisions. These early versions were classified at a lower level, so I was working from incomplete information at first. But when my security clearance was elevated from the level held by governors to the status of cabinet secretary on Inauguration Day, Chertoff's team added more material, and I got the full picture.

The sheer size and complexity of my new portfolio was mindblowing. My head was swimming as I read about the dozens of programs within the TSA alone and the intricacies of air travel safety. Sitting atop the mountain of briefing documents was a half-inch-thick single-spaced glossary of government acronyms. Who knew that NSTAC stood for National Security Telecommunications Advisory Committee? Or that CAPPS meant Computer Assisted Passenger Prescreening System? Or that this almost comically bureaucratic document would prove indispensable? That cheat sheet would be a constant companion during the eventful years that followed, as I acclimated to the players and rituals of Washington. As the aide who delivered the dolly of binders left my office on that December day and the door of my office clicked shut, I looked around and thought, "What have I done?"

A few weeks later, on a freezing but joyous Tuesday, I sat with my fellow cabinet nominees on the west front portico of the US Capitol moments before the inauguration of President Barack Obama. As a US Marine Corps band serenaded the assembled dignitaries, I looked at the crowd below. For as far as I could see, revelers packed the National Mall in a sea of brightly colored hats and parkas that stretched all the way to the Washington Monument.

The atmosphere was both majestic and electric, but already I had a sense of foreboding.

I had learned earlier that day that Chertoff had received intelligence about a possible plot to disrupt the celebration and cause mass casualties. He and his team were monitoring events from a nearby Secret Service command center to make sure none of the threats came to pass. Chertoff and I had agreed that we would wait a day to transition power within the DHS. After being confirmed by the Senate, my swearing in was delayed so that we did not compound our vulnerability with an ill-timed changing of the guard during an active threat stream. As I scanned the hundreds of thousands of cheering people packed in front of the Capitol, I knew that in less than twenty-four hours, I would be the one bearing primary responsibility for their safety. And for the second of what would become many times during the early days of my tenure, the magnitude of my new duties hit me. I wondered what I had gotten myself into.

The Department of Homeland Security was created in part to remedy the lamentable lack of communication and the failure of dozens of government agencies to connect the dots that were so obvious in hindsight in the years prior to the 9/11 attacks—and above all, to protect the public from future disaster. Americans were still reeling from the human loss, from their shattered sense of safety, and from the trauma of witnessing mass murder on television, when President Bush and Congress convened the National Commission on Terrorist Attacks upon the United States in November 2002. Comprised of a bipartisan group of ten of the country's most distinguished and astute leaders, including current and former government officials and leading attorneys and strategists, the commission was tasked with investigating the "facts and circumstances relating to the terrorist attacks"—in nongovernment speak: just what the hell went wrong, who let it happen, and how to prevent it from happening again.

It was critical to identify the fatal mistakes that had become evident during the first year of the investigation and to restore confidence in government's ability to protect the public. The work of repairing the scarred American psyche was also immense. The department was given an ominous-sounding name—Department of Homeland Security—a throwback that felt like it was out of a World War II newsreel.

President-elect Obama asked me to serve as secretary of homeland security after he won the 2008 election. I was an early supporter and helped Obama mount a valiant but ultimately unsuccessful effort to win the late John McCain's home state of Arizona, and I campaigned for him in other states as well. With my background in law enforcement and my experience as a border-state governor, the president-elect thought I was a good fit for DHS, so I agreed to take the job of running this new and sprawling department that everyone warned me was unmanageable, if not downright impossible to run. To me, public service means exactly that: you serve where you are needed. And when the president asks you to serve, you serve. In 2009, the Department of Homeland Security was in its adolescence, and like a teenager, it was gangly and fast growing, with some serious coordination, identity, and communication issues. I saw the challenges, but I also saw the opportunity to make more of an impact than I might have at one of the longer-established agencies.

Everyone in government understood the charge to prevent another attack on the homeland. This never-again mentality set an appropriately high bar for my predecessors, for me, and for future homeland security secretaries. It is impossible to overstate the pervasive confusion, fear, and anger that followed 9/11, and it created a challenging climate to build and manage a giant government agency. A study by the Pew Research Center in 2011, a decade after the 9/11 attacks, found that 97 percent of Americans who were at least eight years old when the attacks happened said they remembered exactly where they were or what they were doing when they heard the news. The recall of the 9/11 attacks surpassed even that of President Kennedy's assassination in 1963. In the 2011 poll, 75 percent of people reported that they'd been emotionally affected a great deal by 9/11, up from the 67 percent who said so a year after the attacks; 61 percent said life in America had changed in a major way since the attacks, up from half who said that in 2002. Note that Americans' anxiety was increasing, not going down, as time went on. This was due in part to the effects of the ongoing wars in Iraq and Afghanistan, as well as the metastatic nature of threats to the homeland—and the media coverage of them—that kept security concerns front of mind.

Reports from late 2001 show a spike in calls to HMOs, increased demand for antianxiety medications, and runs on pharmacies nationwide for the antibiotic Cipro, which had become scarce during the anthrax attacks by US mail in the days after 9/11. Five people were killed and seventeen made seriously ill after coming into contact with a potent biotoxin contained in envelopes mailed to federal government offices, the US Senate, and media organizations, including ABC, CBS, and NBC News; the *New York Post*; and the publisher of the *National Enquirer*, between September 18 and November 21, 2001. Most of the victims were US postal workers and journalists.

The anxiety epidemic had both public health and political consequences. In the weeks after the 9/11 attacks, *Psychology Today* reported a survey that found that nearly half of respondents felt their sense of safety and security had been shaken, and more than half were having trouble sleeping. In another poll conducted by the Harvard School of Public Health and the Robert Wood Johnson Foundation, more than half of those surveyed had taken steps to protect themselves from harm—such as taking precautions when opening mail and avoiding public events.

In the immediate aftermath of 9/11, the anthrax attacks contributed greatly to the national sense of paranoia and dread—and a deepening worry that the enemy had invaded the most mundane facets of American life. This mentality wasn't just held by the ordinary citizen but by those in the highest levels of the US government as well. In October 2001, President George W. Bush speculated publicly and ill-advisedly that "there may be some possible link" between the anthrax-laced envelopes and Osama bin Laden, adding, "I wouldn't put it past him." Vice President Dick Cheney also pointed at bin Laden, saying that al-Qaeda–trained operatives "know how to deploy and use these kinds of substances, so you start to piece it all together." Although the FBI was privately doubtful at the time that terrorists were performing advanced pharmaceutical engineering in the caves of Afghanistan, the agency would not conclude publicly until 2010 that the rare weapons-grade anthrax was mailed by a rogue government scientist at the US Army Medical Research Institute of Infectious Diseases in Fort Detrick, Maryland, who had since committed suicide. Like all of us, Bush was shaken in those early days, looking for answers and lacking conclusive evidence, coming up with some of his own.

The facts as to how terrorists with medieval ideology managed to attack the most powerful nation in the world would eventually be pieced together by the 9/11 Commission, which started its work in 2002. The commission's mandate was staggering in its breadth. It was assigned to assess the roles of intelligence and law-enforcement agencies, immigration issues and border control, the flow of money to terrorist organizations, commercial aviation, budgets, the roles of Congress and the administration. Congress also passed the Homeland Security Act of 2002, establishing a new cabinet-level department, the Department of Homeland Security, and prompting the largest reorganization of the federal government since World War II. President Bush appointed Pennsylvania governor Tom Ridge as its inaugural secretary, a get-it-done former US Marine who had reported for duty in the days following 9/11 as the President's White House Advisor on Homeland Security, not knowing what his job would entail or what resources he would receive to get it done.

Ridge wasted no time in early 2003 standing up the department, which essentially mashed together twenty-two federal agencies and the 180,000 federal employees who staffed them at the time. Placed under DHS command were some venerable institutions, such as the Coast Guard, established by Alexander Hamilton in 1790; US Customs, which had been under the Treasury Department since 1789; and the Secret Service, created by Abraham Lincoln in 1865. Other components that went to DHS had been more recently established, including the Federal Agency of Emergency Management (1979), or brand new, such as the Transportation Security Administration (TSA), established in November 2001; US Customs and Border Protection (CBP) and US Immigration and Customs Enforcement (ICE) were created as part of the reorganization. The logic behind this structure was that combining all of the government's resources to secure under one roof the land, sea, and air borders of the United States, along with the integrity of its cybernetworks, would make the country more resistant to attack and more resilient in its recovery should those defenses be breached again.

When the reshuffling was over, the Department of Homeland Security was a giant hatchling, ranking as the third-largest cabinet agency in the US government, outsized only by the Defense Department and the Department of Veterans Affairs. From just about 180,000 employees and a budget of $33.5 billion in 2003, the first year of its existence, DHS has grown to the behemoth it is today, with 246,000 employees and a $54.2 billion budget for the 2019 fiscal year. The sprawling portfolio of DHS comes with an equally massive oversight apparatus in Congress. When the department was created, there was no corresponding overhaul of the committees that had jurisdiction over the agencies folded into DHS.

The result was lots of redundancy. By some counts, as many as 119 congressional committees, subcommittees, and commissions claim oversight of DHS—and each one of them, it seems, is ready to pounce whenever there is a report of the TSA appearing to treat a passenger inappropriately. Some critics hold up the department as a Frankenstein's monster of government run amok, but having spent years at its helm, I know that a big, complicated country requires a big and sometimes complicated apparatus to handle all aspects of its security. After all, we have seen the chaos that results from a simplistic approach—from zero tolerance at the border to banning certain types of travelers based on their religion, to name a few. These approaches are not only ineffective, but they also come at the expense of our values.

This is not to say I don't understand some of the confusion and ridicule surrounding DHS. Who can forget the early days after 9/11 of the blue, green, yellow, and red color-coded threat matrix, which no one seemed to understand, or the department's recommendation that the public keep duct tape on hand to protect themselves in case of disaster by taping up their windows? I made my own share of personal mistakes too (see "underwear bomber"), and so, no doubt, will my successors. None of this takes away from the fact that the huge, multifaceted department is vital to our nation's security today, even if it does not fit neatly into the boxes that so often define government. One part terrorism prevention, one part intelligence agency, one large helping law enforcement and public safety, and a dash of disaster recovery make for an odd recipe in the traditional political culture of Washington, DC.

The only other institution that was created in a similar big bang fashion was the Department of Defense in 1947, which combined the Department of the Navy and the War Department. Like DHS, the Defense Department was created in the aftermath of an epic triggering event (in this case, World War II), and it was designed to position the United States to lead in the new geopolitical era that followed, the Cold War. Following the 9/11 attacks, the United States was again at the vanguard, this time in the global war on terror. The two departments are alike in one other way. The Department of Defense too had its growing pains, despite having a clearly defined role understood and respected by the American people, an iconic headquarters in the world-famous Pentagon, an awesome arsenal, and an enormous budget. The Department of Defense integrated two agencies (versus twenty-two for DHS), and yet I'll note that after more than seventy years, the Department of Defense is still evolving. In 2018, for example, President Trump proposed the creation of a Space Force as the nation's sixth military branch.

Bureaucracies have a reputation for being static, not evolving. A set of rules and paperwork and hidebound workers don't allow for changing times and the changing dynamics of the world. I get that, but I also know that expertise and systems matter in an organization as huge as the US government. Large, complex organizations require lots of people to make them work. Someone has to handle procurement. Someone has to manage payroll and accounting and IT. And that's just the administrative support necessary to backstop the organization's mission. Where bureaucracies get stuck is in stacking one layer of policy or practice on top of another and losing agility in the process. One example of this would be the hiring process for Border Patrol agents. By the time a person is interviewed, drug tested, and passes a security check, it can take a year to complete the hire. And that's before the agent gets trained and sent to the field. People find other opportunities in the meantime and move on, wasting an awful lot of government resources on a half-finished personnel file.

Government has to evolve to meet the challenges of each era. And the various elements of government have to adjust to each other along the way. I saw this clearly at DHS, which was (and remains) the new kid on the block. At the White House, cabinet secretaries sit around a long oval table with their proximity to the president based on the seniority of their agency. The president sits at the center, with the vice president across the table, and is flanked by the secretaries of state, treasury, and defense and the attorney general. I sat at the very end of the oval, not exactly in a folding chair, though it sometimes felt like it. When the president walks into the House of Representatives to deliver the State of the Union address, the cabinet secretaries line up behind him, again in order of departmental seniority. I was perpetually the caboose.

Protocol aside, I was surprised by the intensity of the growing pains around Homeland Security that were still evident during the early years of the Obama administration. When I took office in 2009, DHS was still not fully incorporated into the country's foreign policy and law-enforcement planning. Storied intelligence and law-enforcement agencies, such as the Secret Service (1865), the Department of Justice (1870), and the FBI (1908), have had more than a century to carve out their turf and their institutional identities. The CIA (1947) and the National Security Agency (1952) were created during the Cold War; the Department of Energy, which manages our nuclear weapons, in 1977. Yet as administrations and global security threats change over time, so do the power positions of the agencies charged with protecting our national security.

Our mission at DHS was so broad that we were neither fish nor fowl: part law enforcement; part intel gathering, sharing, and analysis; part international security policy. Old hands at the Pentagon, CIA, and Department of Justice did not know how to deal with this relatively new department. They did not instinctively prioritize DHS in planning or consult with us in crisis. And because no other federal department has more daily interaction with the public, whenever anything went wrong or looked like it had gone wrong, guess which of us caught the flak from citizens? Headlines rarely resulted from our daily successes in securing borders and transportation, aiding recovery from hurricanes and earthquakes, or improving vaccine supply chains to improve resilience in the event of a pandemic. Little wonder that my aides sometimes jokingly described the DHS as the "Department of Plague and Pestilence."

Appropriate to its status, the department was headquartered during my watch in a ramshackle former US Navy code-breaking compound on Nebraska Avenue, in a residential neighborhood in northwest Washington, DC. The campus lacked the grandeur of more established agencies flanking the White House and the Capitol, and I'll admit to some serious real-estate envy any time I attended meetings at the Department of Justice or the CIA in Langley, Virginia. My employees were crammed into cubicles at the Nebraska Avenue Complex, known as the NAC. There was barely a functioning email system and only the most rudimentary office setup when I arrived. Secretary Ridge had to send staffers to Staples just to buy chairs. When I got to the NAC in 2009, I heard there were still World War II–era munitions stored underground. DHS was scheduled to start moving in 2019 to a facility across the Potomac River on the grounds of Saint Elizabeth's, a onetime psychiatric institution formerly known as the Government Hospital for the Insane. I guess we're making progress?

Today's DHS is not our first go-round with the concept of homeland security. It's just the most recent and largest incarnation of a government function that successive presidents have struggled with for a hundred years. As early as 1916, with aerial combat against civilians emerging as a tactic in Europe during World War I, President Woodrow Wilson convened the secretaries of war, navy, interior, agriculture, commerce, and labor into a Council on National Defense charged with "coordinating resources and industries for national defense" and "stimulating civilian morale." When the United States entered the war in 1917, the council tasked governors with creating their own local councils of defense to shore up the national effort—a precursor to the partnerships I pursued with state, local, and tribal governments in the post-9/11 era. Like many American experiments in homeland security, the council focused more resources on mobilizing the public and the economy for war than on protecting civilians in their homes, schools, and businesses. After the Great War ended, the council was disbanded.

Public anxiety surged again in the late 1930s, with the Great Depression having lowered morale and well-being on the home front and Hitler's aggression mounting in Europe. In October 1938, in the moments after Orson Welles's broadcast of the radio play *The War of the Worlds*, public panic ensued. In retrospect, the gullibility evinced by a science fiction fantasy about Martians invading the Earth may seem far-fetched, but Americans in those years had reason to be jittery—it wasn't unlike the way the country felt in the aftermath of 9/11.

Less than a year after the broadcast, on September 1, 1939, Hitler's army invaded Poland, launching World War II and unleashing violence against civilians on a scale never seen before. Alarmed by Hitler's gains and fearing an expansion of the conflict, President Franklin Delano Roosevelt created the nation's first Office of Civil Defense in May 1941. As director, FDR appointed New York mayor Fiorello La Guardia—another interesting parallel to today, considering former mayor Rudolph Giuliani's role as the public face of New York City's response to the 9/11 attacks. La Guardia warned the president and anyone else who would listen that the American public had never been as vulnerable to an attack as they were in the spring of 1941.

Months later, La Guardia was proved right when the Japanese attacked Pearl Harbor, killing 2,403 American sailors, wounding more than 1,000 others, and drawing the United States into war yet again. Roosevelt tasked his Office of Civilian Defense, modeled on Britain's civil defense program, with preparing Americans for war, much as Wilson had during World War I. But with domestic poverty still rampant, he also wanted to provide social services to support the effort. In a bold gesture at the time, FDR appointed First Lady Eleanor Roosevelt as assistant director of the office, in charge of such nonmilitary tasks as expanding the country's social welfare efforts and volunteer activities in support of the troops. La Guardia dismissed anything that didn't have to do with hardening the country's defenses as "sissy stuff," hardly endearing him to the president's wife. The two would continue to clash over the purpose and the meaning of homeland defense until FDR dismissed them both (perhaps putting more recent White House family dramas in perspective). And in what would become a pattern, the Office of Civilian Defense was disbanded after World War II, leaving our country yet again without a dedicated homeland security apparatus.

Attempts to formalize some kind of homeland security structure continued in fits and starts through the Truman and Eisenhower years and the advent of the Cold War, with national-security considerations at the forefront. Fallout shelters and mass evacuation plans were the order of the day, as Americans came to grips with the prospect of a Soviet-launched nuclear missile capable of reaching US soil. A congressional committee concluded in a November 1957 report titled "Deterrence and Survival in the Nuclear Age" that the United States could not defend itself against a Soviet surprise attack on the homeland. "By 1959, the USSR may be able to launch an attack with ICBMs (intercontinental ballistic missiles) carrying megaton warheads, against which [US missile defense] will be almost completely vulnerable under present programs," the report said. "If we fail to act at once, the risk, in our opinion, will be unacceptable." But there was little consensus regarding whether missile defense was even possible in the atomic age. Another government report projected that 90 percent of the US population would die in a nuclear exchange, leading to the Cold War deterrence doctrine known as "Mutually Assured Destruction."

The undercurrent of dread only deepened in the Kennedy administration as the Cold War kicked into higher gear. President John F. Kennedy implored Americans to protect themselves by stocking fallout shelters and preparing to survive without immediate government assistance. During the Cuban missile crisis in late October 1962, panicked Americans flocked to grocery stores, gas stations, and banks in preparation for an atomic siege. No baby boomer can forget "duck and cover" school drills, diving under their desks, hands clasped behind their heads, as though that would protect them from radioactive fallout. Under President Richard Nixon, the definition of homeland security expanded to include natural disasters, after a government study found that US preparedness was minimal to nonexistent. For the first time, more federal funds were allotted to state governments, who were responsible for the first line of response.

These ad hoc and sometimes uneven approaches to homeland
security continued well into the post–Cold War era, with new government agencies and reorganizations cropping up in reaction not
only to military threats but to nearly every major disaster. After the
1979 near meltdown at the Three Mile Island nuclear power plant in
Pennsylvania, President Jimmy Carter established the Federal Emergency Management Agency (FEMA), consolidating a dozen functions
from fire prevention to the community preparedness program of the
National Weather Service. The Pentagon was given a significant role in
the deployment of the new agency's resources. Progress in homeland
security was undermined for decades, by the recurring tug-of-war
between Congress and the executive branch, among federal, state, and
local governments, between the military and civilian sectors, and amid
a lack of consensus over priorities. Policy was made by a patchwork
of legislation, executive orders, and national-security directives, each
with varying levels of authority, personnel, equipment, and money.

We also learned that creating a new agency does not necessarily mean a president will use it as intended. When the *Exxon Valdez*
spilled 750,000 gallons of crude oil off the coast of Alaska a decade
later, in 1989, President George H. W. Bush sent in the Environmental Protection Agency and the Coast Guard rather than FEMA
to manage the cleanup and recovery. The lack of clear command,
compounded by poor communication and inadequate cooperation
between the federal and state governments and technical experts
from Exxon, resulted in needless delays and massive environmental
damage, generating widespread anger from the public and from Congress. Although the Cold War would end on the elder Bush's watch,
reducing the emphasis on civil defense, it was anything but smooth
sailing for his administration. Calamities came in rapid succession:
Hurricanes Hugo and Andrew in Puerto Rico and Florida and the
Loma Prieta earthquake in California, each revealing government
communication, coordination, and delivery of services inadequate to
the recovery tasks at hand.

Americans' expectations have grown over the years, driving the perception that the federal government rather than the individual or the community is responsible for leading disaster response. This was not the case prior to the 1960s. The journalist John Dickerson writes that as a result, it is no longer enough when a president monitors the federal response from the White House. "He has to dash to the scene. We now expect the president to be a first responder, too." During an unusually severe hurricane season in 1955, President Dwight D. Eisenhower was scarcely mentioned in newspaper stories. "There were no pictures of the former Allied Commander pointing at maps or receiving furrowed-brow briefings from meteorologists," Dickerson writes. Eisenhower, on vacation during some of the storms, relied on local governments, first responders, and the Red Cross to manage. For the government to rush in would send the message that Americans were not up to caring for themselves. "I regard this as one of the great real disasters that threatens to engulf us, when we are unready as a nation, as a people, to meet personal disaster by our own cheerful giving," Eisenhower said in 1957. "Part of the reason is this misunderstanding that government is taking the place even of rescuing the person, the individual, and the family from his natural disasters."

That approach changed with President Lyndon Johnson, who invoked the idea of the president as leader of a national family. After Hurricane Betsy hit New Orleans in 1965, LBJ visited survivors and told disaster officials, "In times of distress, it's necessary that all the members of the family get together and lay aside any individual problems they have or any personal grievances and try to take care of the sick mother, and we've got a sick mother on our hands." LBJ then pushed Congress to fund the recovery. That hands-on approach has set the standard for all presidents since, and each has responded with varying degrees of empathy and success.

When President Bill Clinton took office in 1993, he oversaw a massive restructuring of FEMA, intended to fix some of the shortcomings of the first Bush era. It wasn't long though before the pendulum swung from natural and man-made disaster back to the national-security dimension. The first bombing of the World Trade Center in February 1993 killed six people and left more than a thousand wounded. As a result, Congress identified the mounting threat of terrorist attacks in the United States and in response called for FEMA to develop the capability for detecting and responding to a host of threats now familiar in the post-9/11 era. This "all hazards" approach put under FEMA's purview the responses to terrorist uses of chemical or biological agents or weapons, natural disasters involving critical infrastructure, and even disease widespread enough to affect national security.

Many of the current controversies over the powers, responsibilities, and resources of what those of us in the business call the "homeland security enterprise" are rooted in these earlier attempts by previous presidents. The veering of successive administrations between military preparedness and civil defense reveals confusion, lack of coordination, and most importantly a lack of consistent national strategy that the creation of DHS was intended to fix. The tensions revealed by administration after administration between national security and civil defense, between the responsibilities of the federal government versus state and local governments, civilian versus military control, a reactive versus proactive stance, and the definition of a threat to the homeland have been litigated in this country for literally a hundred years.

This history underscores a pattern of missteps and missed opportunities that are clear mostly in hindsight—and which led to the enormous consolidation that resulted in the Department of Homeland Security. Despite limited exceptions, Americans have long expected and generally received a high degree of safety from their government. And that government, despite its flaws, was able to deliver most of the time. Generations grew up believing they were safe from the government excesses. Safe from persecution, oppression, undue influence in our private affairs—or our elections. Safe to express our opinions, to practice our own faiths, to raise our children according to our own customs, to become educated and acquire property, to better ourselves beyond the lives of our parents.

As a continental nation, buffered by two oceans and flanked by allies along its only two land borders, Americans expected to remain safe from the physical wounds of war on home soil, a sense of security pierced twice, by the Japanese attack on Pearl Harbor in 1941 and again by the attacks of 9/11. Americans felt safe from infiltration by aliens, communists, or foreign powers, except perhaps in *War of the Worlds* or Joseph McCarthy's cruel imagination. We expected to be protected from technology that could do us harm. In the pre-9/11 United States, rockets and jetliners did not rain from the sky, poison was not a weapon of war, and hateful ideology was not piped invisibly into our children's bedrooms and minds—or onto our mobile phones.

The 9/11 attacks and the years that followed shattered that American belief system for millions. The televised massacre of nearly three thousand civilians, followed by the anthrax attacks that began only weeks later, exposed our vulnerability to terrorism on American soil. Then came Hurricane Katrina in 2005 and the financial crisis of 2008, shaking our confidence in the competence of our federal government. The new century brought two endless wars abroad and mass shootings of every sort at home. After the internet's exciting early years as a tool for discovery, connection, and commerce, more of us saw the dark side of the web, a haven for election hackers, data thieves, and lone wolves that has thrown into doubt our most fundamental assumptions about how to keep this country safe, secure, and resilient. And as of January 21, 2009, it was my job to help repair the damage.

CHAPTER 2

Earning My Calluses

My approach to my new role was very much shaped by how I grew up. When I was six, my dad moved our family from Pittsburgh to Albuquerque, to take a job as a professor at the brand-new University of New Mexico medical school. Going from the East Coast to a remote city in the high desert of the Southwest was a culture shock by any standard, even more so in 1964. Albuquerque was first settled in the early 1700s as a Spanish colonial outpost. But it was still taking shape in the 1960s, evolving rapidly from a frontier city of two hundred thousand into a hub of the Cold War science and aerospace corridor linking nearby Los Alamos, where the US military developed the nuclear bombs dropped on Japan to end World War II. My brother and I were up for our Wild West adventure, but for my mom, pregnant at the time with our younger sister, starting family life in the desert was a challenge. I remember her breaking into tears our first night in Albuquerque—the first time I ever saw her cry—as she saw for the first time the adobe house my dad had rented. "You brought us to live in a mud hut!" she wailed.

Fortunately, I come from resilient stock, and within a short time we were thriving. New Mexico was a welcoming place, making it easy for newcomers to get settled and get ahead. It offered opportunities my family would have been unlikely to find elsewhere. As one of only two founding faculty members in the department of anatomy at the medical school, my father was instrumental in shaping the institution. He rose rapidly, becoming dean of the medical school and growing the student body tenfold in less than a decade—lightning speed by the standards of academia. My brother and I loved our newfound freedom, riding our bikes to the mesa, catching blue-tail lizards behind our dad's lab (he paid a nickel for every detached tail), and reveling in an independent yet safe childhood that few East Coast kids could know.

My dad was quirky—and funny. In college, he quarterbacked the Santa Clara Broncos to an upset Orange Bowl win over Bear Bryant's Kentucky Wildcats in 1950. Athlete though he was, he also smoked, and when I was young, he tried to hide the fact from us kids by saying he was going outside to "check the tires." My mom managed to overcome her distaste for adobe and in time even came to love it. After an early career as a university lab technician, where she met my dad, she turned to raising us kids full time once our sister was born. She also became active in the community, serving as a docent and then chair of the board at the Museum of Albuquerque.

At Sandia High School, I played the clarinet in the school orchestra and got involved in student government and the school newspaper. My friends were Latino, Anglo, and Native American. Some were the children of long-settled families and others of immigrants. Some of my friends' parents were not highly educated, while others were scientists with advanced degrees, who, like my dad, streamed to Albuquerque with their families for tech and defense industry jobs at Sandia National Laboratory, Kirtland Air Force Base, and the University of New Mexico. No matter our family circumstances, my classmates and I studied and hung out together and enjoyed the benefits of a decent public education. It wasn't a big deal to me as a teenager, more just the way things were, but I see now how diverse Albuquerque was for its day. I grew up comfortable with people from different backgrounds and life experiences. That ease would serve me well as a future border-state governor and later at the cabinet table.

After graduating in 1975, I headed to California for college at Santa Clara University, a Jesuit college in Silicon Valley and my dad's alma mater. I had become fascinated with government while watching the Watergate hearings on television during high school, especially as a fifteen-year-old, when I heard the rich, deep voice of Texas congress-woman Barbara Jordan delivering the opening statement during the impeachment hearing of President Richard Nixon. Jordan spoke about the US Constitution with such reverence and power; I wanted to take a deeper dive into history and the workings of government institutions.

At Santa Clara, I won a competition for a Truman Scholarship, given to rising college juniors planning a career in public service. I didn't know exactly which direction to go in but was fortunate after graduating with a degree in political science to land an internship on the staff of the US Senate Budget Committee, where New Mexico's Pete Domenici was second to the ranking Republican. My aversion to Nixon had led me during college to identify as a Democrat, but fortu-nately for me, bipartisanship was the watchword of the committee at that time, and Domenici was a longtime friend of my father's. I didn't care that his political leanings were different from mine; there was so much he could teach me, and I was there to learn.

I moved into a tenement-like Washington row house with two roommates on my $400-a-month intern salary and cut my teeth as a federal budget analyst (obviously the most thrilling job in Washing-ton). Within a few months, I was promoted to a staff job analyzing the impacts of tax legislation on the federal budget. Again, not the sexiest job in the world, but the experience taught me there is no better way to understand an organization's priorities than to know where the money flows. That was certainly true at DHS, with its $50–60 billion annual budget, depending on the year, and the perennial tug-of-war between Congress and the department as to how best to spend it.

My year as a Budget Committee staffer gave me intense exposure to the inner workings of Congress. It also made me realize that I would need more education to advance in my career. I applied to law school and chose the University of Virginia because of its national reputation and its proximity to Washington. I loved Charlottesville, made lifelong friends, and enjoyed my legal education immensely, but I always felt drawn back to the West. In my final year of law school, I applied and was selected for a clerkship with Judge Mary M. Schroeder of the US Court of Appeals for the Ninth Circuit. Judge Schroeder's personal chambers were in Phoenix, so after graduation, I loaded everything I owned into my stick-shift, blue Honda hatchback and drove across the country. I arrived in Phoenix on an August afternoon in 1983. I could see the heat waves rising from the desert floor and remember thinking, "Thank God I'll only be here for a year." Little did I know.

Judge Schroeder was one of the few women on the federal bench at that time and became one of my most important mentors. She instilled in me the importance of timeliness, of being succinct, and of understanding the difference between what is interesting and what it important. The latter is a useful skill for two reasons: first, it's a more effective leadership style, and second, it gets more useful things done for more people. I thought about what Judge Schroeder taught me when I confronted the daily deluge of issues crossing my desk at DHS. One minute it was TSA training standards, the next a budget request from Customs and Border Protection, or the Coast Guard needing to upgrade ship's quarters designs before women joined the service. I had to constantly assess what decisions had to be made by me, what could be delegated, and what to put aside. I had to differentiate between what was being debated on cable television versus knowing what was on my desk and what the president needed to see. On CNN or FOX News they might be shouting about body scanners in airports, while I needed to focus on the continuing threat stream from adversaries trying to get explosives onto planes.

Judge Schroeder was an accomplished jurist, but she also understood the importance of work-life balance (before it had that label) and most importantly of having fun, no matter how tough the job. She rarely missed a chance to break out the champagne in her chambers to celebrate birthdays, anniversaries, or one of her clerks passing the bar. I carried that awareness of how important it is to make time for friends and for fun and not waste time on sweating the small stuff throughout my life. It helped later when I was diagnosed with breast cancer at the age of forty-two and underwent a mastectomy. I was able to stay focused during my recovery on the people and things who matter most. Binge reading all of the Harry Potter books also helped.

Phoenix in the 1980s was booming, and the city's law firms were hiring aggressively, offering good money and relatively fast tracks to partnerships. It was also a place where I had quickly forged friendships, and it was halfway between Albuquerque and San Francisco, where I had worked during my law school summers. After my clerkship ended, I joined Judge Schroeder's former law firm, specializing in product liability and commercial transaction appeals. The work was well paid, but it was not my passion. I was still looking for a way into public service. My breakthrough came in 1991, when I was asked by a partner in the firm, John Frank, to join a hastily assembled legal team handling a pro bono sexual harassment case on behalf of a young University of Oklahoma professor who had become involved in the confirmation process of then Supreme Court justice nominee Clarence Thomas. John, a former Yale Law School professor who had also become a mentor, worked on the famous Miranda case ("You have the right to remain silent") and was a national expert on Supreme Court confirmations. He explained that our new client had provided derogatory information about Thomas and that she would soon be called to testify before the Senate Judiciary Committee.

We knew our client's appearance would be newsworthy, but we had no idea how explosive the impact of Anita Hill's testimony would be on American society—and how relevant it would remain to this day. Long before the #MeToo movement, the Anita Hill–Clarence

Thomas hearings marked the first time most Americans had heard the term "sexual harassment." The Hill-Thomas hearings were in many aspects a precursor to the wrenching testimony of Dr. Christine Blasey Ford during the confirmation hearing of Brett Kavanaugh a generation later, including the social and political uproar. As a member of Anita's legal team, I was responsible for assembling a panel of witnesses able to corroborate her story of being harassed by Thomas when he was her boss at the US Department of Education and later at the Equal Employment Opportunity Commission. My witnesses confirmed that the story Anita had told them at the time of the incidents with Thomas was consistent with her testimony before the committee, and they undercut the Republican argument that Anita had recently made up her story to sabotage Thomas. We had more women in the wings prepared to testify that they too had been harassed in the workplace by Thomas. These witnesses were never called, though, and to this day I do not know why. I can only speculate that the senators on the committee were extraordinarily uncomfortable with the subject matter of the hearing and that they wanted to get out of this firestorm as quickly as possible. After three days of hearings, the committee sent the recommendation to pass Thomas's nomination to the full Senate.

The hearings were my first exposure to raw politics and gave me a taste of what it was like to be in the public eye. Our client was treated horribly by the Judiciary Committee, and Clarence Thomas went on to be confirmed to the Supreme Court by a narrow 52–48 margin on July 1, 1991. The obvious injustice of the experience awakened broad outrage and left many voters appalled by the spectacle of a young black professional woman being grilled by a wall of older white men peering down from on high. The Republican members of the Judiciary Committee tried to avoid those optics during the Kavanaugh hearings in 2018 by bringing in a female career prosecutor to question Kavanaugh's accuser, but the ordeal of a woman being forced to recount a traumatic experience on live television and of Kavanaugh forcefully denying the accusations resulted in an appalling spectacle that was damaging for the individuals involved, and for the institutional reputations of the Senate and the Supreme Court. One silver lining that emerged from Hill-Thomas hearings was that the year 1992, known as the "Year of the Woman," saw record numbers of female candidates elected to the US Senate and the House of Representatives. In the wake of the #MeToo movement, it's heartening to see a similar response now, with more women than ever running for office—and winning.

I had taken note of the fact that Arizona's Democratic senator Dennis DeConcini sided with the Republicans, one of eleven Democrats to do so, and had voted to confirm Thomas. I briefly considered running for the US Senate to unseat him, but I decided not to, in large part because DeConcini was an incumbent in my own party, and that seemed like an unwinnable battle. I also liked Senator DeConcini personally and would later appoint him to the Arizona Board of Regents when I became governor. It's important to recognize that even good people will disappoint their friends and make bad decisions from time to time. You may not know it from today's headlines, but public service does not need to be a blood sport.

It was in that moment, though, that I knew I had found my calling. I knew for sure then that public service and politics were where I wanted to devote my energies. I saw how Anita Hill was mistreated, and I saw the composition of the Senate. Our politics had to be better than that. During that time, I became more deeply involved in Arizona Democratic politics and had the job of arranging for Arizona's roll call at the 1992 Democratic convention. It was an incredible thing to watch as we announced our delegate count for the party's presidential nominee, Bill Clinton, in English, Spanish, and Navajo. During that time, I also gained a bit of prominence on the national scene. Two years after the hearings, President Bill Clinton appointed me as US Attorney for the District of Arizona.

I got my baptism as a public figure quickly, when the archconservative editor of the *Arizona Republic*, the state's largest newspaper, wrote a Sunday column accusing me of improper conduct during the Anita Hill hearings and falsely claiming that I had coached a witness to lie on Hill's behalf. His claims were undercut by the official transcript, but of course he did not cite it. I was outraged and embarrassed at this 1993 version of fake news and called my mentor John Frank to complain. He listened to me sputter and fume and then said something along the lines of, "No one is forcing you to go into public service. You made the decision. You need to grow up and get over yourself." And so I did. I developed a thick skin—I earned my calluses—and learned not to waste emotional energy fighting battles that accomplish nothing. While facts do of course matter, making a life in public service means you cannot allow people who disregard the facts to get in your way. Facts are the disinfectant for fake news and should be applied generously and consistently. In the case of the slanderous article, I wrote a tart letter to the editor laying out the facts in the transcript and went on with my life.

I am often asked how I coped with the enormous pressure of my job at DHS. I learned to compartmentalize early. During much of my childhood, my mom dealt with serious physical illness, and during those times, my dad functioned as a single parent, doing all that he could to take care of us kids while also running the medical school. Like many in these circumstances, I became a self-reliant and emotionally contained kid, and those qualities were helpful during a life of public service. I knew to conserve emotion and problem solve in a crisis, to let grievances go and move on when I lost a political or bureaucratic battle. And though I'm not the most effusive person, going through what our family did in those early years helped me to develop a strong empathy for people and a deep desire to help them when they are suffering.

My appointment was confirmed, and not only was I, at thirty-five, one of the youngest US Attorneys in the country, but I was being asked to lead an office of more than one hundred career prosecutors, having never handled a criminal case myself. I had to learn fast, beginning a pattern that would recur over the course of my career. Over the next four years, I supervised the prosecution of hundreds of cases of border-related crimes, putting away drug smugglers and human traffickers, violent criminals in Indian country, and convicting white-collar criminals who had taken advantage of the savings-and-loan debacle of the 1980s. That scandal led to the collapse of hundreds of financial institutions due to improper lending practices that defrauded customers of their savings and cost taxpayers billions in federal bailouts. The savings-and-loan crisis hit Arizona hard and ensnared both of the state's US senators, John McCain and Dennis Deconcini, along with three others, who were accused of intervening on behalf of a political donor, Charles Keating, when his savings-and-loan company collapsed. The Keating case was prosecuted by the US Attorney's office in Los Angeles. In a twist of fate, the lead prosecutor was someone I knew from law school, Alice Hill, who later joined me at DHS.

I also became familiar with domestic terrorism, coordinating the gathering of Arizona-based evidence against Timothy McVeigh for the Oklahoma City bombing and the prosecution of the Viper Militia, a group of white nationalists convicted of plotting to blow up government buildings in Phoenix. The work was deeply meaningful and exciting, but by 1997, I was about to turn forty and found myself casting about for what to do next. The Arizona attorney general's seat would be open in 1998, and I didn't want to be in my rocking chair someday, muttering, "Woulda, coulda, shoulda." I resigned as a federal prosecutor and declared myself a candidate.

Much of my life to this point had been about taking ever larger risks. It was a risk to leave the comfort of New Mexico, where my family had achieved some prominence, for college in California and then law school on the East Coast—a larger risk to leave private practice for government. Now I would take my biggest risk so far by running for office in my own right. It was exhilarating and terrifying. It was also a time of transition for my family. My mom had died a few years earlier, and my dad was getting older and had retired. I had all the signs I needed that life is short, and there's no point in waiting to jump in to the next great phase.

When I first told my dad I was running for office, he was not pleased that I was turning further away from what he saw as a stable and lucrative law career in the private sector, but once he saw how passionate I was, he quickly came around. One of my first campaign contributions came from him, a check bearing the puckish notation "Napolitano Family Trust Fund, exhaustion of principal plus interest." It was in the amount of five dollars. I had never run for anything other than high school class secretary, but I learned to push myself out of my comfort zone, to remind myself that I was running to serve people, and to understand my own strengths and weaknesses as a candidate. One of the first things I did was a poll to see whether I had any name recognition. As a US Attorney for the past four years on some high-profile cases, I thought I would be OK, but the results came back at 8 percent. I'm pretty sure that 8 percent consisted of defense attorneys and felons, and of course, felons can't vote. There's nothing like jumping into your first political campaign to teach one humility. But I found I really liked campaigning, and I got better at it as time went on. I learned to speak less like a lawyer and more like myself. I liked to ask people about what they needed, and most importantly, I learned to listen to their answers.

On Sundays, I would stand in the parking lot in front of grocery stores in those neighborhoods of Phoenix that we knew to be populated by large numbers of independent and moderate Republican voters crucial to winning elections in Arizona and greet people doing their weekly shopping on the way home from church. I'd introduce myself, hand them a palm card printed with my name and important facts about me, and spend a few minutes discussing what they were looking for from their government. In 1998, that meant cracking down on drug smuggling and related crime and enforcing the death penalty, which I am not a proponent of personally, but I recognized my responsibility to enforce it under Arizona law. Interestingly, immigration did not come up on the list of most voters' concerns. These parking-lot meet and greets got to be a ritualistic way of connecting with people—and it worked. I won my first election by thirty thousand votes, helped in part by a brutally competitive Republican primary. Four years later, in 2002, I ran for governor and was elected by a margin of less than 1 percent, which was more typical for a Democrat in a state that tilted very heavily Republican in those days. Even that razor-thin victory was incredibly sweet. In 2006, I ran again, and the situation was different. My name identification was much higher, and I had had a successful first term. I was reelected with more than 60 percent of the vote, carrying every county and legislative district in the state, the first candidate ever to do so in Arizona. My dad was my cheerleader, and the night of my reelection, he treated the campaign staff to turkey sandwiches from Subway. In his exuberance he had violated his own five-dollar campaign spending limit, though I didn't remind him of that.

With the benefit of hindsight, I can see now why so many who knew me when I was younger assumed I would run for political office, but I certainly never thought I would. But I had the good fortune of supportive parents, a great education, and the confidence that comes from growing up in a part of the country with a very mobile social order, where people can rise faster, further, and with less regard to gender, fancy pedigrees, or influential connections than elsewhere. It probably doesn't hurt that I was an overachiever and that my parents took little notice of social strictures for girls, always encouraging me to push boundaries. My dad had a PhD in anatomy, and my mother, a degree in zoology. As scientists, they encouraged curiosity, persistence, and risk taking, traits that I shared and that served me well in public life. Party identity was not important. My mom was a Democrat, and my dad was an independent. He didn't change party affiliations once I was elected to public office. The values in the household were less about party and more about who was doing the most to help other people.

The calluses helped too. When I was US Attorney, the postal inspector did a national child-pornography sting operation, and my office approved nine search warrants against suspects in Arizona but denied a tenth warrant for lack of probable cause. The agent on the case went ballistic and went to the media. There was even an ABC *20/20* episode about the case. There was an accusation that I had not approved the search warrant because the suspect was gay. And since I am a single woman, I must be gay (I'm not). And gays protect gays. When I first ran for governor, we heard that my opponent was getting ready to put these accusations into a campaign ad. This time, instead of squawking in indignation as I had a few years earlier, my campaign manager, Mario Diaz, hatched a plan—which I would learn about after it was underway.

Maricopa County sheriff Joe Arpaio, then already famous but not yet convicted in federal court for racial profiling (or pardoned by President Trump for same), was the unlikely target. As a staunch Republican, though not yet on the party's lunatic fringe, Arpaio made it clear that he would not endorse me for governor. But he also told us that if anyone distorted my record as US Attorney, he would be willing to speak up against them. Arpaio and I had tussled when I was US Attorney over the conditions at the Maricopa County Jail. Working with Main Justice, I'd helped negotiate a settlement that forced him to improve the conditions there, and I believe he respected me for my professionalism and negotiating skills. As soon as Mario heard about the bogus claims involving the one disapproved warrant, he got Arpaio to make good on his offer. We cut a television ad, starting with a siren and then a voice-over by Arpaio: "Warning, warning, warning: this is Sheriff Joe Arpaio warning you that Janet Napolitano has been attacked unfairly." People were so concerned that they started to call into the office to ask what happened and if I was OK, under the mistaken belief that I had been physically attacked. Yes, it was a little bit of political theater, but I believe it kept my opponent from releasing his ad, and I won the race, though I'll admit it is weird that help came from a guy no one would say is my advocate, just as I am not his.

Arizona is a small state but home to more than its share of big political personalities: Barry Goldwater, US senator and failed 1964 Republican presidential candidate, who defined conservatism for a generation; Congressman Mo Udall, a famously funny man with a liberal conscience, whose presidential ambitions were stopped by Jimmy Carter in 1976; and of course, Senator John McCain, who ran for president in 2000 and 2008, losing twice. When I was campaigning for Barack Obama against McCain in 2008, I used to reference Arizona's sad record in this regard and enjoyed McCain's joke that this was one tradition that should continue: "All across America, mothers and fathers tell their children they can grow up to be president—except in Arizona, where they're told they can be runner-up."

I first became aware of McCain when he was running for a house seat in Arizona in 1982, and he was accused in a voter town hall of being a carpetbagger. (McCain was born on a US naval air station in Panama and grew up all over, a navy brat, before attending the US Naval Academy and becoming a naval aviator before he was shot down over Vietnam.) His response was something to the effect that the longest time he had ever spent living anywhere as an adult was as a prisoner of war in Hanoi, which gave me some insight into his backstory. I thought it was a great answer.

It was always interesting to me that the Arizona Republican Party disliked McCain because he didn't check all their boxes. (The state GOP was the Tea Party before there was a Tea Party.) McCain was more conservative politically than people assume, but the fact that he would even talk with Democrats was viewed as a black mark against him. McCain survived an ordeal and came out the other side, seeming fearless. I disagreed with him on many issues, but I respected him, and I hoped he would have said the same about me. As a governor from one party and a senator from another, we both swore an oath to uphold the Constitution, and we approached our work on behalf of Arizonans in the spirit of "let's get on with it."

The place I came from shaped me in other ways as well. Perhaps it matters that New Mexico was the forty-seventh state to join the union and was followed five weeks later by my adopted state of Arizona, the forty-eighth, in 1912. I was lucky to grow up and start my career in these "frontier" states, where women were viewed as capable and necessary partners from the covered wagon days until now. It is no accident that the first woman justice on the Supreme Court of the United States, Sandra Day O'Connor, comes from Arizona. Throughout my career, I was often the first woman to reach a particular milestone, and I get asked about the importance of being a "first woman" this or a "first woman" that all the time: the first female valedictorian at Santa Clara University, the first woman attorney general of Arizona, and the first woman secretary of homeland security. Perhaps not surprisingly, I was the third woman governor of Arizona, the state that has had more female governors than any other. My predecessor and my successor were both women.

This did not spare me from the occasional indignity, though. During my first race for attorney general in 1998, the *Arizona Republic* ran brief profiles of all the candidates for statewide office. Despite the fact that I had served as US Attorney and won several high-profile prosecutions, my identity and accomplishments were considered in a single sentence: "Janet Napolitano is single, says she is not gay." Another time, a reporter asked me, "Do you plan to run as a woman?" Annoyed, I said, "I don't think I have a choice, do I?" The fact is, being the first woman or the only woman to do something is just not something I think about very much in my own career. I am proud though of the larger roles that women are playing in our government, and I am a believer in paying it forward. I hired several qualified women and promoted them into positions of responsibility throughout my career in male-dominated domains, whether in law enforcement or at DHS. What matters is the ability to get the job done. This is true in law enforcement, in politics—and in life. Everyone has to earn their way up, but I believe in helping a qualified person who might otherwise be unrepresented get a fair shot at the starting line.

I met two of my closest women friends in politics, former Michigan governor Jennifer Granholm and former Washington governor Christine Gregoire, when we served as attorneys general in our respective states in the late 1990s, helping to enforce the landmark $200 billion settlement against the tobacco industry. I think what made us formidable as candidates for governor was our experience as the chief law-enforcement officers for our states, a role that traditionally exudes strength, authority, and an ability to protect the public interest. Another of my close friends was former Kansas governor Kathleen Sebelius, who later joined me in the Obama cabinet as secretary of health and human services. Kathleen and I shared our first security challenge in the early Obama administration, managing the response to the H1N1 swine flu outbreak, the first potential pandemic in nearly a century. We worked well together and successfully navigated the country through the crisis. I'm tired of the question almost always asked about any woman in charge (whether out loud or not): "Is she strong enough? Is she tough enough?" By now, we should know the answer.

Here's a case in point. During my first term as governor, prisoners took two guards hostage at the Lewis State Prison in Buckeye, Arizona. The male hostage was injured and let loose after a week, but the female guard remained captive in a control tower, surrounded by police snipers, while our hostage-negotiation teams tried to coax her captors into releasing her. The SWAT team delivered food by robot to reduce the likelihood of casualties, and one day, they accidentally sent a hamburger that was from a different restaurant than the captors requested. I remember clearly what happened next: the enraged captors took a piece of rebar and tried to saw off the guard's finger in retaliation. Our team heard her screaming over an open phone line.

We would have been justified in storming the tower at that point, but my Corrections Department director Dora Schriro felt the hostage would be killed and that others would be killed or injured during the operation. I agreed, and negotiations continued. On Super Bowl Sunday, our negotiators promised to deliver a steak dinner and a six-pack after the game, in exchange for the release of the hostage and the surrender of the hostage takers. It worked. The guard was flown by helicopter to a nearby hospital, and Dora and I greeted her when it landed on the roof. Though badly traumatized, she took us each by the arm and said, "Thank you for not storming the tower. They would have killed me." By the time it ended, the fifteen-day Lewis State Prison uprising was the longest prison standoff involving a hostage in US history. I'm not convinced that a team led by men instead of by a woman governor and a woman Department of Corrections chief would have been as successful. It's of course impossible to know for sure, but I do know that Dora and I made the right call not rushing to use force.

In electoral politics, where there weren't many women, we found it useful to stick together and support each other—as well as to blow off steam and have fun. When I was attorney general of Arizona, my female colleagues and I would find time to have dinner as a group at our annual national meetings of state attorneys general. Our male counterparts would hear about our dinners and ask, "What did you all talk about?" We either said, "Well, about you, of course," or "Our favorite recipes—you know us gals," and shake our heads. During the Obama administration, senior White House women and senior women in the agencies would also meet for regular dinners to offer each other friendship and support. Sometimes we would trade observations about testifying before Congress or trying to get our budgets through the Office of Management and Budget or offer sympathy when one of us had been subjected to the latest unflattering story in the *Washington Post* or the *New York Times* or *Politico*. We were all big girls and had to take it. John Frank would have been pleased.

It wasn't all business: one of the common topics of conversation was our love of jackets by the designer Nina McLemore. They are gorgeous and made of good fabric that doesn't wrinkle when it's shoved in a suitcase during constant travel. We always joked that they are ideal jackets for the woman in the hot seat. We always let newcomers in on this tip—where to get these coveted jackets, which were sold at the time from the living room of a sales rep in DC, not in a store.

Growing up in the Southwest had another profound influence on my view of American life. I have a unique view of how best to secure our country's border with Mexico and fix our broken immigration system. I know from personal experience that the southern border, despite conventional rhetoric, is not and never will be a neat, impenetrable line of demarcation. It is not a Tupperware container but rather a living, breathing membrane, a region where family members live and work on both sides. The border is a vital artery for commerce, agriculture, travel, and tourism, as well as a naturally porous environment for livestock and wildlife, not handily sealed by artificial barriers.

Anyone from a border state who grew up with this reality— regardless of political party—has a different understanding of the facts on the ground than do the many politicians and talking heads who claim expertise. I have walked, flown over, and ridden horseback along our southwest border for years. I appreciate its vastness, as well as the grave consequences of our failed immigration system. It's interesting to me that few of the prominent "immigration hardliners" who dominate the current debate come from border states. As secretary of homeland security, few things annoyed me more than being lectured about the border in front of television cameras by members of Congress from Alabama or Iowa.

I felt confident from day one in my abilities to advise President Obama on border security and immigration. But that was only a sliver of my responsibilities. President Obama was the second president to have a secretary of homeland security, and in choosing me, he had to weigh many factors. His successors will have to do the same, because no one mortal is going to start with all the skills and experience needed to master the most sprawling portfolio in government, save for the president's own. In terms of managing disasters, I worked many times as governor with FEMA and made a practice of partnering the state with local, tribal, and federal governments—a key responsibility of the department. I had plenty of experience managing huge and complex budgets, negotiating with the legislature, and building consensus before making policy. Public health policy? Check. Experience with local law enforcement? Check. My gap was in the international arena. While I knew how to work well with my Mexican counterparts and enjoyed periodic vacations to Italy, where I could explore my family roots and indulge my love of opera, I had not had much exposure to foreign policy.

There is no glossing over my lack of sophistication in this area, and I cringe when I look back on some of it. Shortly after I became secretary of DHS, I was scheduled to go to meetings in Europe, including one with the German interior minister. Mark Koumans, one of the staffers from our International Affairs Office, came in to brief me about my upcoming "bilats." I didn't know that was bureaucratic lingo for "bilateral consultations." Instead, I told him, "I've got my own exercise routine." I really, actually said that. I can't imagine what he must have thought of me in that moment.

The first time someone talked about Yemen, I had to study a map carefully to understand the complex border issue at hand. The terrorist groups were an alphabet soup: AQ (al-Qaeda), AQAP (al-Qaeda in the Arabian Peninsula, the AQ franchise in Yemen), al-Shabaab (the AQ offshoot in Somalia), AQI (al-Qaeda in Iraq), later rebranded ISI (Islamic State in Iraq), now in Syria and known as the murderous ISIS. Mastering the lingo, putting names together with the groups and what threats they pose to the United States took time, and the learning curve was steep. I had to quickly master the history—how did we get here? I also had to master government structures and learn what institutional and personal relationships existed between the United States and other countries. Then there was the intel. How much intelligence cooperation did we have with allies, and how much were we trying to achieve?

I knew, as I had earlier when I became a federal prosecutor, that I had to get up to speed fast—and I did. I came in overconfident. After all, I was a two-time governor; I got myself elected as a Democrat in a red state three times, once in a landslide. I thought, of course I can come in and run a government department. It was only when I got there that I came to understand the job was much larger and much more complex than running a state. As a leader, having a little humility is key. It's important to recognize what you know and what you don't and surround yourself with people who have experience in the areas that you lack.

Fortunately, I had excellent guidance from the career staff at DHS and some from the State Department. Rand Beers, a former US Marine Corps officer and diplomat, who is one of our country's top antiterrorism experts, became one of my most trusted and relied-upon advisors. Heidi Avery, a veteran national-security expert and deputy homeland security advisor to the president, quickly became a key asset and ally to me at DHS. I found another strong member of my team in John Cohen, a law-enforcement and homeland security expert who advised me when I was governor and whom I appointed as chief operating officer for intelligence and analysis. I find that government works best when there are personal relationships built on trust. I had a few connections in the White House from my work with the Obama campaign and knew the president's chief of staff, Rahm Emanuel, as well as his senior political advisor, David Axelrod.

Things could have been dicier with the State Department under the leadership of Hillary Clinton. My last real conversation with Hillary had been during the 2008 campaign, when she called after the

Iowa caucus, furious that I planned to endorse Obama. "You can't do this!" she yelled. (There may have been a modifier thrown in there.) I explained that I had tried for months to reach out to her campaign and was disappointed, especially as I was the first woman chair of the National Governors Association, that there had been no response. And my interactions with Obama had convinced me that he was the type of leader who could bring healthy change to Washington. I got off the phone by assuring Hillary that I would support her if she was the nominee. It's fair to say that relations between us were never warm from that point on. But we both made sure that our personal feelings did not affect the work of our departments. The State Department became a vital partner on several global initiatives, including our Blue Campaign against human trafficking; the Merida Initiative, a partnership between the United States and Mexico to fight organized crime; and humanitarian initiatives, such as extending temporary protected status to immigrants from distressed countries like Haiti and El Salvador (both of which were rescinded by the Trump administration in early 2018).

One of my key allies in foreign affairs was John Brennan, a longtime CIA official who served in President Obama's first term as deputy national-security advisor for Homeland Security and Counterterrorism and later became director of the CIA. The president routinely convened his national-security advisors for weekly meetings in the White House Situation Room, dubbed "Terrorism Tuesdays," during which cabinet secretaries and senior military and intelligence leaders went around the table, providing updates on what was going on in our respective agencies. I did not find the meetings terribly productive and was not the only one who felt this way, but we all understood the importance of giving the president as complete a picture as possible of the counterterrorism activities of the US government in one sitting. One of the great shortcomings identified by the 9/11 Commission had been the government's practice to silo vital intelligence by agency, depriving the commander in chief and the national-security team of a 360-degree perspective on existing and emerging threats to the United States.

The meetings were not my style, with time spent on briefing the president and each other, as opposed to problem-solving. It didn't feel like the best use of time, for instance, for me to brief the generals and intelligence types at the table about the complex immigration history of the Boston Marathon bombers, when they had wars to fight and we all had terrorists to stop. And President Obama had a signal when he was getting impatient—he would lean back in his chair, eyes half closed, as if to say, "I know this already; tell me something I don't know." Some may have perceived this as arrogance, but I saw it as an understandable reaction by a man with a thousand things on his plate and a limited amount of time. He didn't need to have repeated to him what he had already read and absorbed. We just knew that when we saw this move, it was best to make your point quickly and move on. Tedious though these roundtables were, this is what good government looks like. Such exercises don't make for exciting ratings, and they may not even make the news, but they do ensure that the senior players are all on the same page and can avoid the confusion we so often see from the Trump administration.

Beyond Terrorism Tuesdays, Brennan and I found it helpful to consult one on one to make sure DHS was in sync with the White House on key issues. We made a point of meeting for breakfast regularly at a Greek diner in Adams Morgan, one of Washington's trendy neighborhoods, where we would discuss over spinach-and-feta omelets ways we could work together more effectively. Homeland Security was still a relatively new cabinet department and had never been run by a Democratic administration. I used these breakfast meetings to ensure that Brennan and by extension the White House were up to speed on the issues confronting the department that did not make it onto the typical national-security agenda. These ranged from funding challenges for a new fleet of Coast Guard Legend Class cutters to the department's role in protecting the government, consumers, and businesses from increasingly frequent cyberattacks. Brennan and I chose our spot because the service was fast, the food was good and cheap, and the diner was near empty when we met, affording us the necessary privacy (a consideration this administration doesn't seem all that concerned about).

With support from these key colleagues and an expert career staff, I covered a lot of ground in a short time. My goal was to make sure my intel briefings were just that—brief—and with key information and key people only. That was not the case in my first intel briefing on my first full day as secretary, a spectacle that started at 7:00 a.m., with me weaving through a squirrel's nest of old filing cabinets and World War II–era detritus in the basement of DHS headquarters and into a windowless room, the Secure Compartmentalized Information Facility, or SCIF. All eyes in there were on me as each member of my new senior staff delivered a readout on topics from the president's daily brief, the overnight intelligence report distributed early each morning to top national-security officials (which I came to think of as the "Who's Trying to Kill Us Now?" report).

Though well meaning, most of that prolonged initial session, with far too many people in the room, was not helpful. This was a typical example of what I think of as "security theater," a sense of apparent motion that is reassuring to those performing their lines but does not necessarily advance the homeland security mission. I had no time for that. I saw plenty of security theater during my time in Arizona (and made a few cameos myself), but none of it compared to the award-worthy performances I would see on Capitol Hill and cable news shows in the years to come. I am not suggesting that all security is theater or even that all theater is bad—very often, the public (and the bad guys) need to see an armed security presence in key places such as borders and airports. But much of the political rhetoric is counterproductive in the security sphere, and the best security is most often delivered quietly, to the point, and behind the scenes.

I quickly decided that my morning intel briefings would be limited to myself and my two designated CIA briefers, along with Rand Beers, undersecretary of the national protection and programs directorate; Caryn Wagner, my undersecretary for intelligence and analysis; and my chief of staff, Noah Kroloff. You can get a lot more done with five people in a room than twenty. These more private sessions gave me the opportunity to ask questions and to probe the intel for evidence of new and emerging threats that the department needed to prepare for. Sometimes the briefings took thirty minutes, sometimes a full hour. And they were daily: on weekends, the CIA briefers would come to my condo, and when I was on vacation, my Coast Guard military aide would securely deliver the briefing books to wherever I was staying. The president's daily brief was the opposite of security theater. It was the nuts and bolts of ensuring that all the top security advisors were getting the same intel as the president, leading (theoretically at least) to more and better coordination across the sprawling security enterprise of the federal government, another key recommendation of the 9/11 Commission.

These were the building blocks of the job. I think people might be surprised to learn how little chest beating, saber rattling, and flag hugging contribute to their actual security and how much it is enhanced through competent management. It's not as entertaining, but I'm telling you it works. We are made safer through the unseen, uncelebrated work: unifying two dozen agencies into a single, new department; fixing weak spots like FEMA; streamlining operations to save money; informing and negotiating with Congress; collaborating with our military, intelligence, and law-enforcement agencies; and partnering with state, local, and tribal governments. We help the public most by communicating candidly and quickly, providing facts and valuable emergency advice over emotional and often inaccurate political rhetoric, no matter how dramatic it sounds. As former governors, Kathleen Sebelius and I practiced the same rules while leading our respective federal agencies: tell them what you know, and tell them what you don't. Don't conceal. Don't duck and cover. Maintain your credibility.

Pennsylvania's Tom Ridge, the first secretary of homeland security, was also a former governor and brought a similar mind-set to DHS about plain talking and the importance of working with local governments and first responders. (And he had that low-ego pragmatism that allowed him to send a staffer to the office supply store with his credit card so that the people charged with waging the new war on terror would have chairs to sit on.) I give Secretary Ridge great credit for getting the department up and running under the most trying conditions. Michael Chertoff, the second DHS secretary, came from a background of public service at the federal level. He was a former US Attorney and then head of the Criminal Division at the Department of Justice, who was later appointed to the federal bench by President George W. Bush. Chertoff gave up a lifetime appointment to take over DHS, and his particular talent was putting into place effective early systems to share intelligence about travelers, trade, and cargo.

My successor, Jeh Johnson, came to DHS from the Pentagon, where he was general counsel, leading a ten-thousand-attorney legal shop. While Jeh continued many of the initiatives I had undertaken, he also had his share of crises to deal with, including the sudden increase of unaccompanied children from Central America in 2014. Former US Marine Corps general John Kelly, who served as President Trump's first secretary of DHS, brought deep military and counterterrorism experience, but his brief tenure before becoming White House chief of staff precludes a meaningful assessment at this time of his impact on the department. Kelly's former deputy in the White House, Kirstjen Nielsen, became DHS secretary in 2018. A self-styled cybersecurity specialist who also had worked in DHS during the Bush administration's response to Hurricane Katrina, Nielsen did not have the leadership experience typical for a cabinet secretary. She had no background in immigration policy or law enforcement and stumbled badly in managing the family-separation debacle caused by the Trump administration's zero tolerance policy at the US-Mexico border in 2018.

When I looked around President Obama's cabinet table, you cannot imagine an administration more different in terms of culture than the one we have at the time of this writing. It was filled with people who had significant background in public policy: Health and Human Services Secretary Kathleen Sebelius of Kansas and I were former governors; Energy Secretary Steven Chu was a Nobel Prize–winning nuclear physicist; Education Secretary Arne Duncan was an accomplished school innovator in Chicago; Secretary of State Hillary Clinton and Interior Secretary Ken Salazar from Colorado were former US senators; Defense Secretary Robert Gates and CIA director Leon Panetta, who later succeeded Gates, had decades between them of serving presidents from both parties. My colleagues were enormously qualified people with significant records of achievement. And they were nice to each other! One of my favorite activities is white-water rafting, a sport that involves collaboration and trust in an environment that can go very quickly from being fun to stressful—not unlike public service. When it comes to working with any group of people, I always ask myself, "Are these people you'd like to do the river with?" I was always happy to do the river with these people. We worked well together, and we would never, ever throw each other overboard to score points with the boss.

Obama set the tone. He conducted himself in a very presidential way, demonstrating dignity, restraint, and decency in terms of both his professional and personal conduct, and he raised the bar for us. People called him "no-drama Obama," and that was who he was. We never had to worry about conflicts of interest or the appearance of such conflicts, not only because we and our deputies were thoroughly vetted but also because we would never dare disappoint or embarrass the president who had placed his trust in us. This has nothing to do with politics. Every president deserves officials who will carry out his or her policies, but no president until now has demanded that they go around the table in front of the cameras, swearing their allegiance to him. It was embarrassing for me to watch the members of President Trump's cabinet do that early in his term. I cannot imagine what that must have felt like, with the world watching. Or, for that matter, being fired by tweet.

From my perspective, there are two additional qualifications one must have to serve effectively as secretary of homeland security. One is the ability to compartmentalize, so you don't become overwhelmed by the sometimes terrifying information you know. The DHS secretary cannot be curled up in a ball under her desk when important decisions need to be made. The other, frankly, is a dark imagination—to be able to get inside the mind of a potential terrorist to predict next moves or understand the potential loss of life in the case of a massive pandemic. Those two traits may seem to be at odds with each other, but they really aren't. Fortunately, I suppose, I seem to have them both.

In my new role, I started nursing a lot of what-if scenarios in my mind: What if the H1N1 virus, circulating in early 2009 among livestock, turns into a pandemic and threatens millions? What if terrorists manage to get bombs on a plane? Or planes? What if there is an attack on a subway station or the Super Bowl? What if there is a massive cyberattack crippling our energy grid or our financial system? What if not just one but three hurricanes make landfall at once (a scenario I was horrified to see come to pass in 2017)? What if there are coordinated terrorist attacks on multiple cities, one at a time, or multiple attacks on the same city? How would you respond? Who would you call? What measures would you put in place? How would you work with the White House? I will say, one thing that never occurred to me during my tenure was the possibility that there could be a cyberattack on our democracy itself by a foreign adversary. I would have never guessed that my imagination just wasn't dark enough to see that coming.

The ability to compartmentalize necessarily involved finding time to myself to decompress, which was difficult during that time. Some nights after leaving my office late at night, I would try to unwind with a swim in the pool of my condo building. This was the time I could put everything going on in the world out of my mind for an hour and recharge. Sometimes I used that time to digest the high volume of information that came at me rapid fire in any given day, especially if I had a particularly difficult problem to untangle. I could devise solutions and process the responsibilities, the challenges, and, above all, the unknowns. The answers did not come readily. And the questions felt more urgent by the day.

CHAPTER 3

Mission Impossible?

When I wake up in the morning, the first question I ask myself (other than "Where's my coffee?") is "What is the mission?" Not only what needs to get done, but what's the end goal of each project? I'm sure it's a byproduct of my experience in law enforcement. I want to know the facts and figure out what to do with them. One frustrating aspect of the DHS, though, is that so much is unknown. While scenarios are easy to design, our responses were not. Each scenario has many variables that can change in an instant. I could never know how prepared we really were for particular dangers until they manifested themselves and we were put to the test. And I grappled with the disquieting reality that there was no way we could contemplate every threat. Not to mention that when I started at DHS, we simply didn't have a reliable playbook for something like a pandemic or for a disabling cyberattack on critical infrastructure or for decentralized, simultaneous attacks on cities around the country involving a biological, chemical, or nuclear agent. There was work to do.

By 2009, the Department of Homeland Security was six years old, and my staff and I were running at full speed, moving from one crisis to the next. It's difficult to overstate the degree to which we were inventing the job as we went along in those days or how hard it would be to find adequate time to focus on proactive planning. Sometime during my first few weeks as secretary, I came upon the department's mission statement, which I found mechanical and frankly uninspiring. It said the DHS was focused on "preparing for natural disasters and terrorist attacks through planning, technology, and coordinated efforts. In the event of a natural or man-made disaster, DHS will be the first federal department to utilize a full range of state, local and private partnerships to alleviate the effects of a potential disaster."

I know this impulse to edit may strike some as an exercise in navel-gazing or mindless bureaucracy, especially with terrorists to catch, borders to secure, and disasters to fix. I was certain, though, that without deeper clarity about our mission and how our role was distinct within the federal government, it was going to be tough for the many DHS employees I led to work together toward a common goal. The very first step had to be the creation of a mission statement that we would all rally behind. When I took office, the department was comprised of nearly a quarter million federal workers who had been thrown together in the aftermath of 9/11 and who came from two dozen agencies, each with its own priorities and ways of doing things. We had to start rowing in the same direction.

I began by studying some of the mission statements laid out by other departments. It seems like common sense, and it is standard practice in the private sector to lay out goals and ways to measure progress, but I know you'll be shocked to know that common sense doesn't always abound in government, at least not without a prod. It turns out that a 1993 Clinton-era law requires every major federal agency to define its mission. For the Department of Defense, the mission is pretty straightforward: "to provide the military forces needed to deter war and to protect the security of our country." For others, it's a bit more complicated. The mission of the Department of Energy, for example, is "to ensure America's security and prosperity by addressing its energy, environmental and nuclear challenges through transformative science and technology solutions." Rather vague and all encompassing. The mission of the Environmental Protection

Agency is "to protect human health and the environment." No one would argue with that, but according to what principles? This one misses the mark.

Missions matter. Missions are important for what they say and for what they leave out. In 2018, for example, the US Citizenship and Immigration Services (USCIS), a component of DHS, removed the reference from its mission statement about the United States being "a nation of immigrants" and replaced it with one emphasizing "protecting Americans." In its entirety, the former mission statement read: "USCIS secures America's promise as a nation of immigrants by providing accurate and useful information to our customers, granting immigration and citizenship benefits, promoting an awareness and understanding of citizenship, and ensuring the integrity of our immigration system." The new mission statement reads: "US Citizenship and Immigration Services administers the nation's lawful immigration system, safeguarding its integrity and promise by efficiently and fairly adjudicating requests for immigration benefits while protecting Americans, securing the homeland, and honoring our values." I find it telling that the statement emphasizes "protecting" Americans from legal immigrants rather than the value of legal immigration, which touches most families in this country. It's no wonder the zero tolerance debacle flowed from this type of thinking.

As we sat down to develop our mission statement, we began by figuring out what, aside from sheer size and complexity, was unique about the Department of Homeland Security. The taxpayer might reasonably ask, "Why does someone patting me down at the airport report to the same cabinet department as the commander of a Coast Guard cutter or a disaster response expert from FEMA?" And honestly, I did too in those first months. Americans have long differed on the optimal size and value of their federal government and on the competence of its workforce, but no one can deny that it is a behemoth, with 2.8 million civilian employees in more than four hundred agencies plus another 2 million in the uniformed armed forces and reserves. But these civil servants don't wake up one day and decide to move around the boxes to make themselves feel useful. They are responding, as they did after World War II and again after the 9/11 attacks, to a changing world with new challenges and threats.

The Department of Homeland Security was designed to be a critical player in the country's defense, intelligence, law-enforcement, and emergency response. Yet unlike the rest of the national-security apparatus, the department's primary responsibility is to local communities. We see the American people as our key partners rather than our charges. My team and I started by recognizing that no government agency, even one as huge as ours, could take the place of an empowered and vigilant public. We had to dispense with the traditional attitude of not panicking the public. As a former governor, I agreed with my FEMA administrator Craig Fugate, who said, "If you don't tell the public what is going on, that's the recipe for panic." In nearly any emergency, whether it is terrorism or a natural disaster, neighbors and bystanders can reach victims a whole lot faster than can the federal government, or any government, for that matter.

No federal agency, even one that has at its disposal the massive resources of the US Customs and Border Protection, Immigration and Customs Enforcement, FEMA, the Transportation Security Administration, the Secret Service, the Coast Guard, and a sizeable intelligence and analysis arm, can substitute for knowledgeable local community leaders and well-trained first responders. One of my mantras quickly became "Homeland Security starts with hometown security." As a governor, I saw many times that people in affected communities are more critical navigators in a crisis than the feds who may outrank them on some organizational chart. At DHS, we wanted to empower American communities to help solve problems rather than simply waiting, with a victim's mentality, for the federal government to fix it. I think this is what President Eisenhower feared when he declined in 1955 to become the face of hurricane relief. And we have endless examples of American ingenuity and determination to help each other without waiting for the government. Think of the "Cajun Navy" in Houston after Hurricane Harvey in 2018—hundreds of Louisianans driving their pontoon boats through the streets of their neighboring state, rescuing people. Or celebrity and humanitarian Bethenny Frankel, who organized and funded a private airlift to deliver relief supplies to Puerto Rico following Hurricane Maria.

Especially from the vaulted halls of the federal government, it's easy to lose sight of the importance of local leaders and first responders. One Sunday in early May 2011, I was touring Alabama and Mississippi, checking on our response to a succession of tornadoes that had killed 348 people over the course of three days. As I was asking survivors what we could do for them, a member of my security detail rushed over and told me I was needed immediately on the secure phone in my vehicle. It was John Brennan in the White House Situation Room, who informed me that US Special Forces were on their way to Pakistan to apprehend Osama bin Laden. I spent the next several hours engaged in a surreal balancing act, commiserating one moment with tornado victims, then hustling the next back to the secure line in my black Chevrolet Suburban for top-secret updates on the bin Laden mission. I wasn't the only one compartmentalizing. Many people now know that while President Obama was cracking jokes at the White House Correspondents Dinner, he was aware that US commandos would soon be on their way to capture bin Laden.

Late that afternoon, as I sat in the back seat, parked on a small country road in Smithville, Mississippi, Brennan called and confirmed that the mission was over and that bin Laden had been killed. He also told me that President Obama would address the nation from the Oval Office within a few hours, but before doing so, he planned to inform a few key foreign leaders. While the president stepped out to make those calls, I asked the others on the speaker phone in the Situation Room whether anyone had thought to call the governors of New York, New Jersey, or Virginia or to alert the mayor of New York City. Not surprisingly, no such calls had been placed or contemplated, even though these jurisdictions had suffered the greatest losses of life in the September 11 attacks.

In the crush of everything else going on, the importance of giving a confidential heads-up to our own local leaders simply didn't register. National-security considerations would not permit us to get ahead of the president and say what exactly had happened, but I thought it was important to alert certain elected officials of a significant news event so that they would know to have their media shops on standby, be prepared to address their constituents, and give local law enforcement time to get ready in case public reaction got out of hand. As a former state leader, I knew it was something I'd have wanted. I volunteered to make the calls, and to this day, I remember the gratitude in Mayor Bloomberg's voice when I told him to watch the president's upcoming television address, which had not yet been publicly announced. Even on a secure line, I couldn't tell the mayor over the phone that bin Laden was dead, but Mayor Bloomberg is a smart man, and he immediately realized that only something of major importance like that would necessitate a Sunday evening call at home from the secretary of homeland security. "Thanks for letting me know, Janet," Bloomberg said. "I was about to go to bed."

Another difference between DHS and other agencies is the sheer amount of engagement we have with the public. No other agency of the federal government has more touch points—literally, in many cases—with the people we serve. The Transportation Security Administration is the one most Americans know, and yes, I am aware that their view of its 42,000 agents in blue latex gloves is far from favorable (more on this later). Consider also the 350 million people who encounter our US Customs and Border Protection officers each year when they leave or enter the country, US Citizenship and Immigration Services for the privilege of becoming a naturalized citizen, or Immigration and Customs Enforcement when they run afoul of the law, our FEMA agents when disaster strikes, and even our Science and

Technology laboratories, whose unseen work protecting our food and water supplies from bioterrorism keeps them safe every day.

While other intelligence and law-enforcement agencies operate in secrecy out of necessity (and sometimes out of inertia), at DHS we make a point of doing our work in public, to the greatest degree possible. The Department of Homeland Security is paradoxically the most seen and heard yet the least understood of the federal agencies. Our open approach means there is no shortage of spectators with perfect hindsight, criticism, or ridicule (just Google "don't touch my junk" or "duct tape and plastic sheeting"), but it's important for people to understand that we are all in this effort together. The goal is to empower them to think of themselves as problem solvers, not as potential victims.

The third feature we identified in the DHS ethos is an organizational culture that places a high value on civil liberties. Although the department's reach is global and our work is central to the national security of the United States, the DHS plays by home field, not battlefield, rules. That means it doesn't have the latitude of the military, the CIA, or other intelligence agencies, who, when operating internationally, are not constrained by the US Constitution and its prohibitions, for example, against unreasonable search and seizure or self-incrimination (though they may be constrained by other treaties and rules). I know there is much controversy surrounding the discussion of privacy and security, especially how best to achieve one goal without harming the other, and this relationship deserves thoughtful exploration and a fair debate.

When Congress authorized the Department of Homeland Security in 2002, lawmakers from both parties recognized the fear that Americans would sacrifice too much of their personal privacy in advancing national security. Congress wrestled with similar concerns in the months following the 9/11 attacks, when it passed the USA PATRIOT Act, dramatically expanding the federal government's surveillance abilities. The public was understandably anxious about terrorism. At the same time, Americans are traditionally suspicious about the expansion of government power, and one of this scale was unprecedented, except during times of war. The legislation gave law enforcement powerful new surveillance tools to be used within the United States to detect and disrupt terrorist cells here and abroad. It also required more extensive—some would say, intrusive—vetting of travelers and cargo.

In response to these concerns, Congress required the new Department of Homeland Security to include an Office for Civil Rights and Civil Liberties, as well as a Privacy Office under the direction of a chief privacy officer, the first for a federal agency. The Privacy Office was charged with assessing our practices and procedures so that we were always striving to incorporate concepts of privacy into our security planning from the outset. Privacy principles were tested during the Obama administration, with controversies over things people could see, like full-body scanners in airports, as well as those they could not, such as the collection of personal data by intelligence and law-enforcement agencies. Few people know that DHS has offices dedicated to civil liberties and privacy. But it does, and the people who run it are vital to ensuring that DHS is asking itself the tough questions and identifying policies that properly balance competing interests.

It is ironic that I was tagged "Big Sis" on the Drudge Report, where reports of DHS excesses, most of them inaccurate, popped up and were fanned by other right-wing media sites. "Big Sis Wants to See under Your Clothes" blared a typical headline about airport scanners. "Big Sis Issues Turkey Warning" read another, after I implored flyers to leave their Thanksgiving leftovers on the plate and not cram them into their carry-on bags, creating an additional and messy screening job for our overtaxed workers. The label was sort of funny at first— after all, what better signals that someone has arrived in Washington, DC, than being given her own nickname? Of course, almost everyone has a nickname these days, most of them conferred on people by President Trump himself. Back then though, the "Big Sis" gag contributed to what I think was an unwarranted fear of an Orwellian state hiding behind the cloak of national security to violate Americans' civil rights and to usurp power in violation of the Constitution. Looking back, I wish I had responded more forcefully to the false claim rather than assuming people would see how unfounded, even absurd, it was.

Out of this far-reaching examination of our responsibilities, we came up with the Department of Homeland Security mission "to help create a safe, secure, resilient place, where the American way of life can thrive." Note that we didn't say we could completely prevent disaster, whether caused by humans or nature, but that we would, when such events inevitably did happen, help communities prepare and recover better and faster than the US government had previously. This isn't intended as fine print or an evasion; it is a recognition of the risks we must accept to maintain an open society. It's a tall order, and I question some of the risks we tolerate. But I remain confident we can strike the right balance between national security and protecting Americans' constitutional rights, even as I believe this is an area for continuous vigilance and improvement.

I got a taste of the fine line we walk in that regard a few months later. In April 2009, DHS released a report to law-enforcement agencies on right-wing extremism, noting that domestic terrorists "may be gaining new recruits by playing on their fears about several emergent issues." The report cited the election of the nation's first African American president and the Great Recession as catalysts for right-wing radicalization. In a footnote, the author defined right-wing extremism as "those groups, movements and adherents that are primarily hate-oriented (based on hatred of particular religious, racial or ethnic groups), and those that are mainly anti-government, rejecting federal authority in favor of state or local authority, or rejecting government authority entirely." It also referred to the possibility that disaffected veterans returning from Iraq and Afghanistan were at risk of right-wing terror recruitment and were prized for their combat skills. Timothy McVeigh, the Gulf War army veteran convicted of killing 168 people in the 1995 Oklahoma City bombing, was cited as an example.

The report had been commissioned during the Bush administration, and I had not reviewed it before it was published in the first months of the Obama administration. This was not unusual, given the change of administrations, to allow the career staff to complete projects already underway. But the ensuing uproar taught me some valuable lessons. Some people seized on the comment about veterans and portrayed the report as saying that troubled veterans were potential terrorist recruits frothing at the mouth. How things are written really matters. Even a poorly worded phrase can distract from the overall message, such as the need to better understand what conditions "could" lead "some" veterans to become violent extremists, in an effort to do a better job at prevention. But the veterans' groups were furious, as were some members of Congress, and I understood. I apologized publicly and pulled the report, so it could be rewritten. But lost in all of this was the report's tragic prescience. Several recent mass shootings in the United States have involved men between the ages of twenty-five and forty-seven who learned to operate weapons in the military. It was true of the shooter who killed eleven at a bar in Thousand Oaks, California, in 2018; the one who killed twenty-six in a church in Sutherland Springs, Texas, in 2017; another who killed five police officers in Dallas in 2016; and the one who killed twelve service members and civilians at the Washington Navy Yard in 2013—among more than a dozen such episodes over the past decade.

President Obama never spoke with me about the uproar over the report, because, as I discovered, he has a unique ability to focus on larger issues and not to sweat the smaller ones. Nonetheless, some of his White House aides got torqued about the DHS findings, in part because they wanted to get ahead of the standard suspicion that a Democratic administration wasn't being supportive enough of the military, and they were intent on having good relationships with the veterans' community. Obama believed that actually protecting and caring for veterans is much more important than racking up political points. Beyond that, the Department of Homeland Security is a major employer of US veterans, and we consider their training and service extremely valuable to our mission. But I can understand why these facts were drowned out at the time and contributed to the mistaken perception that we did not have veterans' best interests at heart.

We will never know what impact, if any, a more deftly worded warning may have had in averting the epidemic of mass shootings that followed. The honest answer is probably not a whole lot. One government report cannot undo a knot that confounds law enforcement, national security, and elected and public health officials. To this day, I view the demise of that report as the triumph of political correctness over an otherwise valuable analysis. It was also emblematic of a larger truth. As Americans, we far too often end up undermining our own interests because we are unwilling to address our own blind spots.

Our acceptance of combat weapons in the hands of civilians is just one example of such a blind spot. Others result from a misreading of the threat landscape. For instance, the widely held view is that terrorism in the United States is a threat posed predominately by radical Islam, when in fact the Government Accountability Office reported in 2017 that 73 percent of violent incidents resulting in death since September 12, 2001, were perpetrated by white supremacists and right-wing extremists. The report received next to no media coverage. Later, in an unrelated statement, President Obama was derided for stating that far more Americans died falling in their bathtubs than they did from terrorist attacks. Maybe he didn't choose the most felicitous comparison, but the point that radical Islamic terrorism occupies a singular and static threat in the eyes of the American public is worth noting. Unceasing dread, of course, is what terrorism is about.

Another misunderstanding of the threat landscape can be found in the poisonous debate over who should be allowed to enter the

United States: different groups cherry-pick one set of immigration statistics over the other, depending on their biases. Whether people come from Mexico, the countries of Central America, Muslim-majority nations, or those in Africa, it is possible to weave numbers into any kind of story. And the resulting gaps between what is real and what is feared raise critical questions about how best to direct our limited intelligence and law-enforcement resources.

Blind spots abound. Most people have unrealistic expectations of what the government can do for us in a crisis. One of my goals during my tenure at the DHS was to move from the victim model to one of resilience. One of the aspects of the job I felt most passionate about was empowering citizens so that we think of our country not as a collection of 325 million potential victims but as 325 million potential partners. The "victim model" leads people to overestimate what local and federal governments can do in a crisis and to underestimate what they can manage on their own. Victims are dependent on overwhelmed first responders for safety in times of disaster, when their property is destroyed by wildfires, hurricanes, tornados, or earthquakes. But if people and communities take necessary precautions, make a survival or recovery plan, and are prepared to be on their own for seventy-two hours following a massive disaster, our resources can be allocated in the most effective ways to save the most lives and help keep as many people comfortable as possible. This doesn't mean that DHS should neglect citizens, like the horror show that occurred in Puerto Rico, where, as of this writing, American citizens are still suffering months after Hurricane Maria and it is becoming clear that the storm's official death toll was dramatically understated.

Passivity and complacency are not traits typically associated with the American spirit, but there is a shocking lack of preparation in our communities, even for predictable natural disasters. We see further carelessness when it comes to cybersecurity, on the part of individuals, businesses, and governments. As consumers and citizens, they count on companies and government to secure their personal data online, a calculation many users of Facebook and other social media platforms are only now rethinking in the wake of the Cambridge Analytica scandal. And many Americans, including elected officials, have infuriatingly turned a blind eye to preparing for the biggest and most irreversible risk of all, climate change.

There is no greater contradiction between our expectations and our actions than on the topic of immigration and border security. No one questions that our country, and every country, for that matter, is entitled to enforce its borders and determine who can be a legal resident or become a citizen. We all agree that the US immigration system is broken. The question is how to fix it. Currently there are eleven million undocumented people living in the country without a path to legal status. But the policy questions that underlie those rights are as raw and unsettled as they have ever been: Where do we put our border-enforcement resources? How much legal immigration do we plan for? How do we build an immigration system that's comprehensive and fair?

To have any hope of success, we have to break down the misinformation that has been spread for years by politicians, unelected extremists, and the media who carry their remarks. Before "zero tolerance" and "family separation" entered the lexicon, many Americans were understandably confused by inflammatory rhetoric. Despite President Trump's repeated and false claims, the United States does not have "open borders," and most Democrats do not advocate for an open-border policy.

And while it is popular to insist that those who enter the country illegally "get in line" behind those who entered legally, there really is no line. Country quotas cause profound imbalances in the supply and demand of visas for certain countries and for certain types of workers. The delays are extreme for people trying to enter legally from countries with high demand: Mexico, China, India, and the Philippines. A US permanent resident's adult son or daughter will have to wait roughly twenty-one years (that's not a typo) to file an application for an immigrant visa if they're from Mexico, according to the State Department's visa bulletin, published monthly. In 2018, there were nearly five million people throughout the world waiting just for permission to apply for permanent-resident status. Once that permission is granted to a fortunate few, it takes at least six months to vet the application and five years of lawful residency in the United States to be allowed to apply for citizenship. You can see why people don't think they have a chance to enter legally.

We hear a lot about "border security," a term also subject to manipulation. It refers both to the physical borders and to the area from the physical border to approximately one hundred miles into the interior of the United States, where the majority of the population lives. US Border Patrol agents work in the one-hundred-mile zone and are free to stop anyone and inquire about their immigration status. It is true that immigrants cross the US-Mexico border illegally, but the numbers are at a forty-year low. And most of those who enter unlawfully are from Central America, not Mexico. A large proportion of these migrants claim humanitarian status. To stop this traffic, President Trump has proposed building a wall or other physical barrier along the length of the 1,954-mile border, from San Diego, California, to Brownsville, Texas, at a cost estimated from $12 billion to $38 billion.

Americans should know that the border is already secured by roughly seven hundred miles of fencing and wall, the deployment of sensors and cameras, air patrols both manned and unmanned, and the activities of roughly 18,600 US Border Patrol agents. Border security is overseen by US Customs and Border Protection (CBP), the largest federal law-enforcement agency, under the Department of Homeland Security, with over 40,000 agents. To give you an idea of the size of the force, the FBI employs approximately 35,000 special agents and support specialists. I am not suggesting that the CBP is too big, as they have a huge and demanding mission very different from the FBI's, but I can tell you that Trump's executive order adding 5,000

Border Patrol agents is not going to result in equal value in terms of additional border security. Nor will sending US troops, as Trump did in the days prior to the 2018 midterm elections.

The real personnel shortage is in immigration judges who can resolve the cases of those prosecuted for entering the country illegally. The nation's immigration courts are presided over by administrative law judges, who are responsible for adjudicating removal proceedings as well as for processing applications for asylum and refugee status. Deportation is a civil, not a criminal, proceeding, overseen by an administrative law judge, not a judge appointed under Article 3 of the US Constitution. There are about 350 immigration judges staffing sixty immigration courts spread across communities throughout the country.

During the first year of the Obama administration, Attorney General Eric Holder and I wrote to the director of the Office of Management and Budget (OMB), Peter Orszag, suggesting that the budget for immigration be viewed holistically: from DHS, which handles border security and immigration enforcement, to the Department of Justice, which manages the immigration court system. We wanted to link funds for hiring more Border Patrol agents to funds for hiring more immigration judges. Orszag was not convinced, and we never succeeded in persuading OMB to link immigration enforcement with the adjudication of immigration cases. We now have a backlog of about seven hundred thousand immigration court cases. At the current rate, it would take more than two years to adjudicate these cases, assuming no new ones are added. This, of course, is not a reasonable assumption.

The term "catch and release" is another political hot potato, referring to the practice by which once undocumented immigrants are apprehended, agents enter their data into the CBP system, and then they are transported across the US border without an actual deportation order having been obtained. If they are caught coming back, the US government has a record of their prior illegal entry and can charge them with illegal reentry, a more serious offense. The purpose of this exercise is to avoid housing undocumented immigrants in severely overcrowded detention facilities inside the United States at an additional cost to US taxpayers, while they wait for a bail hearing.

The term "interior enforcement" refers to efforts beyond one hundred miles of the border to enforce our nation's immigration laws, primarily by arresting and detaining people suspected of being in the country illegally and presenting them for deportation to the nation's immigration courts. Once picked up and detained, the majority of immigrants post bail and are freed and are given a report-back-by date for a hearing. Arrest and detention is managed by Immigration and Customs Enforcement (ICE), under the Department of Homeland Security. Applications for citizenship, asylum, or temporary protected status are handled by US Citizenship and Immigration Services (USCIS), also under the Department of Homeland Security.

As the public became aware during the family separation crisis of 2018, managing the border is complicated. Responsibilities are divided among federal agencies, primarily the Department of Homeland Security for border security and immigration enforcement and the Department of Justice for adjudication of immigration cases and prosecution of cross-border crime. And within the Department of Justice, there are different lines of jurisdiction, depending on the type of cross-border criminal we are dealing with. In cases involving drug smuggling, we have the Drug Enforcement Administration (DEA); for human trafficking, we have the FBI; and for weapons smuggling, the Bureau of Alcohol, Tobacco, Firearms and Explosives (ATF).

This legal matrix is inherently complex. I understand how easy it is to misunderstand the phrases and how this in turn leads to a larger and dangerous misunderstanding of the issues. These phrases are weaponized in the media and contextualized incorrectly to scare people who are told undocumented migrants are "invading" and "overrunning" the United States. On the other side, it is an overstatement to characterize all immigrants as fleeing desperately dangerous conditions and seeking a better life for themselves and their children.

Of course, not all those crossing the border are angels; there are definitely some bad actors here, and they should be dealt with according to the law.

Perhaps the biggest political football of them all is the concept of "comprehensive immigration reform." It's a plan to fund improved border security, streamline and clarify the nation's current visa system, and provide criteria under which most of the current 11.2 million unauthorized immigrants in the United States could get right with the law and earn a pathway to citizenship. Comprehensive immigration legislation passed the US Senate in 2013, but the House did not take it up. In fact, Congress has not passed a comprehensive bill of this nature since this Immigration Reform and Control Act of 1986, during the Reagan administration. That law allowed unauthorized immigrants to apply for legal status if they met certain conditions, granting amnesty and putting 2.7 million immigrants, one quarter of the total number today, on the path to citizenship. The law made it illegal for an employer to knowingly hire an unauthorized immigrant, but due to lax enforcement, it had the unintended consequence of fueling the market for fake documentation.

We made real progress on border security during the Obama administration, but we never achieved our goal of comprehensive immigration reform. As I learned from our early stumble on the report about violent right-wing extremism, the White House was sensitive to the Republican story line that, as a Democrat, President Obama would be seen as "soft" not only on the military but also on crime and immigration enforcement. Regarding the latter, the narrative remains that Democrats, in attempting to woo Latino voters and appease immigrant advocacy groups, a key constituency, are prone to lax enforcement of our immigration laws—the specious "open borders" claim.

In fact, the trend under Obama went in exactly the opposite direction. Several factors came together early in Obama's first term that led to a considerable increase in the number of border apprehensions and deportations over the Bush years. First, thousands of Customs and Border Protection officers and US Border Patrol agents authorized by Congress and hired during the Bush administration completed their training and were ready to deploy after President Obama took office in 2009. The number of agents assigned to the southern border increased from around 15,000 in the final year of the Bush Administration to 17,500 under Obama. Second, we increased the number of removal proceedings for those we apprehended rather than turning them back at the border, further enhancing our border security statistics. Total removals increased under Obama as well, from 359,000 during the last year of the Bush administration to 387,000 in 2010, the first full year of the Obama presidency.

By demonstrating real progress on border security, we believed Obama would gain enough credibility to negotiate comprehensive immigration reform with Republicans in Congress, including a path to legal status for the eleven million or so undocumented immigrants already in the United States. The thinking was that if we showed our commitment to securing the border, Congress would be more open to reforming our broken immigration system, which readily refreshed the supply of undocumented immigrants. Clearly, it was a mistake to assume logic would prevail. That calculation failed to have any effect during the Bush administration, the Obama administration, and now, it appears, the Trump administration.

Of course, we learned quickly that no matter what we did, Congress would find a way to carry their narrative forward. The president was excoriated for not being tough enough on immigration, and he wasn't the only one. I remember a particular moment when I was sitting before the Senate Judiciary Committee in 2013. Jeff Sessions, then a senator from Alabama and the hardest of immigration hardliners before he became attorney general in the Trump administration, was berating me for not being tough enough on undocumented immigrants. Meanwhile, in the back of the hearing room, a group of so-called Dreamers were yelling at me for being *too* tough and splitting up families.

I despaired that Congress would ever be able to pass anything resembling immigration reform, much less comprehensive reform. To do that will require dealing with facts, not stereotypes, reducing the overheated rhetoric from our political leaders and showing why immigration reform is in everyone's best interests. It's better for security, our economy, and our place in the community of nations. But so long as comprehensive immigration reform remains a toxic set of talking points by both left and right, we won't get there.

For our part, we missed critical opportunities to communicate with the American people. Maybe it wouldn't have made a difference, but we should have been more clear about what we were doing to secure the southern border and why we chose to penalize employers rather than low-wage workers in our efforts at interior enforcement. We did this because we wanted to get the most bang for our law-enforcement buck by also cracking down on labor and safety violations when making arrests. We were trying to institute real priorities within Immigration and Customs Enforcement and to do so with an awareness of the limited resources available to us along the most traveled land border in the world. We were, of course, very interested in slowing and deterring the amount of illegal immigration over the southern border, which we did. And we were also committed to immigration reform.

In 2018, revulsion over the Trump administration's forced separation of parents and children at the US-Mexico border in the wake of its zero tolerance policy led to calls to abolish Immigration and Customs Enforcement (ICE). This is not the answer and represents an oversimplification of the problem. ICE has national-security functions in addition to immigration enforcement, including the apprehension of cross-border criminals and terrorists, which must continue. Instead, ICE needs clear priorities so that it focuses on those who have committed serious crimes in addition to an immigration violation, known gang members, and identified national-security threats. Just as the Drug Enforcement Administration does not arrest every person it finds with a bag of pot, or the Department of Justice does not prosecute every bad check case, ICE should prioritize its use of federal resources (meaning tax dollars and agents' time) to best protect the country.

When I was secretary, instituting priorities was not universally popular with ICE agents, and we worked hard to communicate the importance of our policy to the fingertips of the agency, meaning units in cities around the country. When the priorities were effectively abolished during the early days of the Trump administration, we saw an uptick in cases of arresting parents who were dropping off their children at school or of undocumented immigrants who were themselves the victims of crime or were longtime residents who owned homes and businesses, paid taxes, and had no criminal record. Such actions are indiscriminate and unwise—and cruel. ICE agents who spend their time on such cases cannot devote their time to more serious matters. With respect to ICE, the solution should be to mend it, not end it. Our country needs both border security and effective immigration enforcement. Our efforts should be strategic and targeted, recognizing that not all undocumented immigrants merit the same treatment.

Without the same prominence given to messaging about immigration enforcement and border security as the administration gave to health care, a vacuum may have been created that left Democrats and Republicans in Congress to duke it out and for talking heads to shout past each other in the media, twisting the narrative. Enlisting the American people in an informed discussion was not a big enough part of the equation, an error the consequences of which are still being felt today.

The president was occupied fully during the first two years of his administration by the financial crisis and his health care initiative.

And sometimes even a boiling pot like immigration reform gets put on the back burner. At one point in those early years, Obama's chief of staff, Rahm Emanuel, approached a small group of cabinet secretaries who were chatting informally at the end of a meeting, after the president had left the room. "I hope you all understand," Emanuel told me and the others. "I don't care what you all have on your plates. Nothing happens until we get health care done."

We got the message. Every presidency has its priorities. Some are tied to the particular issues about which that president is passionate, like passing a comprehensive health care bill; others are situational, as in the case of the desperate need for economic recovery. In light of the imperatives of the time, President Obama could not do everything at once. I did give speeches and have meetings with the president where we discussed ways to fix our immigration system. But nothing we had to say fit on the brim of a baseball cap. Obama is a sophisticated, nuanced thinker, and he could not persuade enough people with his sophisticated and nuanced message in the political and media environment during his first term. Even a president cannot break through with facts, challenges, policies, and problems for which people have no appetite. We would not demagogue on immigration, and as a result, we did not break through and fix what was broken.

When the Democrats lost their majority in Congress in the 2010 midterm elections, we effectively lost our ability to enact comprehensive immigration reform. It didn't help that Republicans kept moving the goalposts. It was easy for them to say that they would not engage in immigration reform until we demonstrated "operational control" of the border. But by 2013, we had pushed illegal crossings (as measured by apprehensions) to forty-year lows, constructed 750 miles of fencing or wall, installed ground sensors along the entire border, begun border-wide air surveillance, and operated a series of checkpoints within 100 miles of the border.

By "operational control," what they meant was that they would not engage in any bipartisan immigration reform effort until we could demonstrate that no one *ever* crossed our southern border illegally. Given my deep knowledge of the border, I know this is a ridiculous standard and one that ignores the relationship between our immigration policy and those seeking to cross the border illegally. We need to make it easier for people coming to work in specialized industries to obtain a visa and cross legally through our ports of entry. We need to help unify families. And we need to face reality.

Drive through the San Joaquin Valley in California, as I recently did, and you'll see Help Wanted signs from growers desperate for a workforce to harvest their crops. If President Trump ever succeeds in his massive wall-construction project, where will the labor come from to build it? If you need someone to stay with an elderly parent twenty-four hours a day, who do you think will be available to hire?

We have a strong demand for workers in agriculture, construction, and home care, not to mention the high-tech visas at the other end of the labor spectrum. By unduly limiting the number and types of visas for those coming to work, we create an incentive to cross illegally—or to overstay a visa. This is one of the many reasons that immigration reform must be comprehensive to be effective.

There is another way in which President Trump's controversial zero tolerance policy had unintended consequences. It's true that someone caught crossing the border illegally has committed a crime, but it is a federal misdemeanor for the first offense. We have lots of crimes on the books, but we do not always have the resources to prosecute each one, without making trade-offs. As a federal prosecutor, I wouldn't throw the book at small bad check cases; we focused on the money launderers instead. Choosing to prosecute every illegal entrant criminally means that federal prosecutors are removed from handling things like drug smuggling, human trafficking, and gun running cases that impact the safety of those living near the border, in favor of prosecuting misdemeanors. Because children can't be held with adults in criminal custody, they must be separated from their parents. In short, while "zero tolerance," like "operational control," may be nice sound bites for a political base, it results in a terrible misallocation of resources and a needless humanitarian crisis.

The Trump administration's family separation debacle in the summer of 2018 was entirely self-created. An illogical policy was made even worse by incompetent management: the failure to plan under zero tolerance for entirely predictable questions about how DHS, the Justice Department, and HHS would coordinate their responsibilities in apprehending undocumented immigrants; how to handle a surge of prosecutions; and how separated children would be cared for, tracked, and reunited with their parents. It was compounded by incoherent, uncoordinated communications from the White House and the federal agencies, resulting in confusion on the front lines, the needless misery of children, public revulsion, and an international outcry. This is government malpractice, and we should not tolerate it, regardless of our political differences.

Perhaps the mess will open some people's eyes to the complicated nature of managing an international border and the benefits comprehensive immigration reform would provide. I can only hope that voters will reward candidates who speak honestly and pragmatically about our need for immigrant labor and our values of keeping families intact. In this, as in so many things, elections matter. They really do.

CHAPTER 4

Freedom and Fear

Late in the evening on October 3, 2001, the House Judiciary Committee was wrapping up debate on a bill to authorize expanded surveillance powers in the three-week-old war on terror. There were questions about some of the provisions requested by President George W. Bush to enhance the government's abilities to prevent future terrorist attacks. Committee members asked about the ease with which investigators could eavesdrop on telephone, internet, and financial communications. They wanted to know how information could be shared between local law enforcement and federal intelligence agencies like the CIA. There were questions about the potentially intrusive surveillance of consumers by their internet service providers. As the evening wore on, though, the official record shows the concerns being dismissed nearly as quickly as they were raised. Ground Zero was still smoldering. Like most Americans, members of Congress were struggling with shock, grief, anger, and, most of all, the fear that there was more to come. In that environment, who would vote against a law titled "Provide Appropriate Tools Required to Intercept and Obstruct Terrorism"?

At 8:30 p.m. on that Wednesday, after six hours of debate, the committee voted 36–0 in favor of the PATRIOT Act, moving the bill to the full House. The next day, Bush authorized a covert program of warrantless domestic surveillance under the National Security Agency. The program was intended to get around some of the limitations established by the 1978 Foreign Intelligence Surveillance Act, which prohibits the government from eavesdropping inside the United States without first getting a warrant from the Foreign Intelligence Surveillance Court. That same morning, October 4, 2001, letters laced with deadly anthrax spores would start appearing in the mail rooms of news organizations and federal government offices along the East Coast.

Despite the fact that many lawmakers were unable to read the bill (their offices were closed in the days that followed due to the anthrax scare), the PATRIOT Act sailed through the House of Representatives and went to the Senate, where it passed 98–1, on October 25, 2001. Wisconsin Democrat Russ Feingold was the only member of the US Senate to vote against it. "I recognize that this is a different world with different technologies, different issues, and different threats," Feingold cautioned before casting his no vote. "Yet we must examine every item that is proposed in response to these events to be sure we are not rewarding these terrorists and weakening ourselves by giving up the cherished freedoms that they seek to destroy."

Few were in a mood at that time to hear warnings about government overreach. The war on terror was a global effort, and there was broad consensus that the government needed a vast expansion of its surveillance powers against a stateless enemy, an unknown number of whose fighters were believed to have infiltrated the United States and were lying in wait in "sleeper cells" to attack. On October 26, 2001, Bush signed the PATRIOT Act into law. "The bill before me takes into account the new realities and dangers posed by modern terrorists," Bush said in the East Room of the White House, flanked by congressional leaders, Vice President Dick Cheney, Attorney General John Ashcroft, FBI director Robert Mueller, Pentagon chiefs, and other members of his cabinet. "It will help law enforcement to identify, to dismantle, to disrupt, and to punish terrorists before they strike."

The PATRIOT Act reflected the grim mood taking shape in this country after the attacks, as shock was channeled into rage, and the still-open wounds evolved into determination to prevent any future attacks, whatever the cost. And it was intended to address the challenges outlined by President Bush in his deeply emotional speech to a joint session of Congress nine days after the attacks. "Americans should not expect one battle, but a lengthy campaign unlike any other we have ever seen," Bush said at the Capitol, before an audience of lawmakers, New York governor George Pataki, New York City mayor Rudolph Giuliani, and the New York City Police and Fire Department commissioners, as well as family members of victims. "It may include dramatic strikes visible on TV and covert operations, secret even in success. We will starve terrorists of funding, turn them one against another, drive them from place to place until there is no refuge or no rest. And we will pursue nations that provide aid or safe haven to terrorism."

Then came one of the most famous lines of his presidency. "Every nation in every region now has a decision to make," Bush continued.

Either you are with us or you are with the terrorists. From this day forward, any nation that continues to harbor or support terrorism will be regarded by the United States as a hostile regime. Our nation has been put on notice: We're not immune from attack. After all that has just passed, all the lives taken and all the possibilities and hopes that died with them, it is natural to wonder if America's future is one of fear. Some speak of an age of terror. I know there are struggles ahead and dangers to face. But this country will define our times, not be defined by them. As long as the United States of America is determined and strong, this will not be an age of terror. This will be an age of liberty here and across the world. Great harm has been done to us. We have suffered great loss. And in our grief and anger, we have found our mission and our moment. Freedom and fear are at war.

Bush's speech was precise in its language and tone, intended not only to assure the American people their government was up to the challenges of the post-9/11 era but also to set the world on notice that the United States was a changed nation, with consequences for allies and adversaries alike. "Whether we bring our enemies to justice, or bring justice to our enemies, justice will be done," Bush said. Members of Congress abandoned the tradition of partisan applause, as the entire chamber rose again and again to express support for the president. "There was no glitz or glamour in his speech—there was no table thumping, no roaring that 'we'll go out and get these people,'" former representative Vern Ehlers of Michigan told a US House of Representatives historian, "just a straightforward laying out what our country faces." House Minority Leader Richard Gephardt of Missouri announced that Democrats would decline to deliver the response message traditionally given by the minority party after a joint session. "We want enemies and the whole world and all our citizens to know that America speaks tonight with one voice," Gephardt said.

The strengths of our young homeland security enterprise—and our failings to date—are rooted in this determined mind-set that took hold in the weeks after the 9/11 attacks. Among its many far-reaching impacts, the PATRIOT Act set in motion the expansion and reorganization of the national-security and intelligence agencies that in 2002 would be combined within the new Department of Homeland Security. While concerns about potential government overreach via the PATRIOT Act were raised, most notably by Feingold, the dissent was easily overshadowed by the urgency of the moment. Writing in *Newsweek*, journalist Fareed Zakaria identified some of the early tensions already apparent in 2002: "We have been here before. America has a long history—some of it good, some bad—of trying to ensure the security of its citizens against mortal threats from within. Nothing in our present crisis suggests that we need throw away that history, those lessons or our fundamental belief that liberty can indeed be balanced with security. The question is how to do it this time."

Zakaria pointed at a law-enforcement apparatus that already seemed dangerously bloated and inefficient, noting, "When the Department of Justice sends out one of its now routine terror alerts, they go to 18,000 law-enforcement agencies around the country. Have you ever wondered why we have 18,000 law-enforcement agencies? The crazy-quilt structure of American government, with local, state and federal authority, overlapping agencies and shared powers, is the single greatest threat to America's safety. It's difficult to organize and reorganize government to meet this new challenge. It's easy to show resolve by rounding up foreigners, fingerprinting people and asserting new powers." Civil liberties groups were alarmed over provisions of the PATRIOT Act that permitted the indefinite detention of immigrants and other noncitizens. Businesses were concerned about the potential monitoring of e-commerce transactions, then just beginning to grow.

As we assess the progress of the Department of Homeland Security during its second decade, these early concerns deserve another look. The PATRIOT Act was intended to modernize surveillance practices and to break down the silos within government that led to the catastrophic intelligence failures preceding the 9/11 attacks. And the 2001 version of the law did much of that. It transformed the culture of law-enforcement and intelligence agencies, making investigating terrorism their top priority. It updated surveillance laws written, as Bush noted, "in the era of rotary telephones," to include email, internet, and cell phone communications.

In 2001, fax machines and Blackberry pagers were the tools of the day. Google's search engine was only three years old, and there was not yet a browser for the dark web, where terrorists and their sympathizers could connect. The first iPhone was six years away. Twitter would be created in five. In 2002, American cell phone subscribers sent an average of thirty-five text messages a month—about one a day—using their "multitap" keyboards. Yet it was already clear in the immediate aftermath of 9/11 that traditional law-enforcement and intelligence agency tools were being outmatched by communications technologies available at that time to the public. The PATRIOT Act expanded the reach of federal search warrants, allowing law-enforcement agencies to obtain warrants valid across all districts and states, since electronic communications at this point routinely crossed state and international boundaries.

The PATRIOT Act also changed laws on information sharing, allowing government agencies to gather "foreign intelligence information" from both US and non-US citizens, a practice that would later lead to explosive revelations by Edward Snowden, a government contractor turned fugitive, of domestic spying by the National Security Agency. Under the law's controversial Section 215, the government was permitted to obtain "business records relevant to a terrorism investigation," an exceptionally broad scope. In 2001, critics from civil liberties groups warned that the government's powers would become so vast that investigators could force public libraries to turn over an individual's borrowing records.

In June 2013, the covert warrantless surveillance program that Bush had initially authorized in 2001 blew open. Snowden leaked information to the *Guardian* newspaper revealing that the National Security Agency had used Section 215 authority to collect customers' cell phone data from such companies as Verizon and Sprint, capturing credit card data and the phone records of US citizens. The Snowden revelations prompted worldwide outrage against the US government and within the United States as well. In their wake, a coalition of strange bedfellows emerged in multiple lawsuits filed against the PATRIOT Act, and there was also an unlikely role reversal between Congress and the Obama administration. The author of the PATRIOT Act, Representative Jim Sensenbrenner, a Republican from Wisconsin, filed a brief in support of the ACLU's lawsuit claiming that the NSA program amounted to "one of the largest surveillance efforts ever launched by a democratic government" and was causing a fundamental breach of Americans' constitutional rights to privacy.

The Obama administration responded that the collection of all phone call metadata in the United States was conducted in the "public interest" and did not breach the constitutional rights of Americans. Before the lawsuit and others like it could be resolved, Congress passed the USA Freedom Act of 2015, requiring the NSA to stop its bulk collection of telephone metadata and instead to submit search orders with local service providers. In this respect, the revelations by Snowden caused legitimate questions to be raised about the collection and retention of data concerning US persons by the US government. But I strongly disagree with the way Snowden went about making these revelations known. There are established procedures for whistleblowers within the government and protections for them that are strongly enforced. How ironic is it that Snowden is exiled in Russia, a country that has involved itself deeply in the democratic processes of the United States?

While questions of overreach may seem obvious, easy, or even fashionable to pose now, in the life-or-death, us-or-them climate that prevailed following 9/11, the imperative to stop terrorists above all was consuming and largely nonpartisan. It was and remains the primary responsibility of the US government to keep its citizens safe. Equally important, however, is examining how the homeland security apparatus created in those weeks and months has grown, at what cost, and to what effect. Is the current homeland security structure adequate in an age when an attack may not result in collapsed buildings but in collapsed faith in our democratic institutions? Is the giant statutory response contained in the PATRIOT Act effective today?

The answer in both cases is no. The 2016 attack by Russia on the infrastructure of our democracy reveals new vulnerabilities not anticipated in the law. In 2018, the Trump administration confirmed earlier reporting by US intelligence agencies that Russian hackers had penetrated voting systems in more than thirty states. The outcomes of that penetration are still unknown, most notably whether voting totals were affected as a result. Russian entities were also responsible for millions of surreptitious political ads on Facebook, targeted at users whose data was collected by a political consulting firm working for the Trump campaign, Cambridge Analytica, which went out of business after the revelations.

Data is being collected, processed, analyzed, and shared at an increasing rate and in ways not anticipated when the PATRIOT Act was first written. Businesses want to be efficient and to satisfy the public's desire to consume data. Technology makes it possible. We are used to having our internet behavior tracked by cookies. Now we are tracked in real life too. Mundane tasks and daily living—reading, cooking, exercise, using electricity, listening to music or watching TV, home security monitoring, and a person's precise location in the home while doing all these things—can generate data. Much of this activity is recorded and stored by companies that make these technologies, but it is not analyzed by the government. People are entitled to a reasonable expectation of privacy under the Constitution, even if they choose as consumers to sacrifice that privacy by using these internet-enabled devices.

Professor Woodrow Hartzog, a prominent scholar in data protection law, uses the phrase "fixation of a moment designed to be fleeting" with regard to surveillance. The amount of data being generated is great, as is the desire to analyze it. But the vast majority of the data is not relevant to any investigation. Nonetheless, there are significant parts of the government (and definitely the private sector) that will want to ingest and analyze that data. More data sources result in more noise and reduce anyone's ability to distinguish a seminal moment from a fleeting one.

In the 2001 *Kyllo v. United States* decision (involving infrared scanners to see whether a homeowner was using marijuana grow lamps), the late US Supreme Court justice Antonin Scalia posited that one of the questions the court used to determine whether the search was unreasonable was asking whether the device the government used was generally available to the public. When "the government uses a device that is not in general public use . . . [then it is] unreasonable without a warrant." We would all agree that the devices the general public use today are very different than they were when Justice Scalia wrote those words nearly two decades ago. And as technology has evolved over that time, the amount of data collected using that technology has increased exponentially. The court will be hard-pressed to rely on its "general population using the technology" test to determine whether a search is unreasonable.

The exponential growth of technology also affects how the Supreme Court views the Fourth Amendment and unreasonable searches and seizures. There is a judicial doctrine called the "third-party doctrine," which states that individuals do not have a privacy interest in their private data that they share with third parties. In Justice Sotomayor's concurrence in *United States v. Jones* (decided while I was secretary at DHS), she wrote, "It may be necessary to reconsider the premise that an individual has no reasonable expectation of privacy in information voluntarily disclosed to third parties. This approach is ill-suited to the digital age, in which people reveal a great deal of information about themselves to third parties in the course of carrying out mundane tasks."

In 2018, in *Carpenter v. United States*, the Supreme Court held that the government could not access cell site location information without obtaining a warrant. The court determined that cell phones and the services they provide are "such a pervasive and insistent part of daily life" that using the cell phone necessitates sharing of information such that the user did not voluntarily assume the risk of turning over a comprehensive dossier of his physical movements. The data we are collecting and generating warrants appropriate protection.

Sometimes that data has important security consequences. In 2017, the Pentagon was alarmed to learn that US service members were inadvertently revealing the locations of secret military installations, as well as their daily routines, through the data on their Fitbits and GPS-enabled fitness apps. One online heat map displayed the data of US personnel training on a US naval facility on Diego Garcia in the Indian Ocean. Another published the exercise routines of US troops in Niger, not far from the location where US Special Forces troops were killed in an unrelated ambush. At other times, the data is banal but has broad implications. A couple in Portland, Oregon, were surprised to find out that their conversation was captured by their self-activating Amazon home speaker and emailed in an audio file to the man's employer. The husband and wife revealed to the media they had been talking about hardwood floors, but it's not hard to imagine how much damage a home eavesdropping device could have done if shared inappropriately.

About a year after I became secretary, I attended a breakfast meeting at a Washington, DC, hotel hosted by the *Christian Science Monitor*. I was asked about a recent article, again by Fareed Zakaria, in which he charged that the US government had overreacted in its response to the 9/11 attacks. Zakaria noted that in nearly a decade since September 11, 2001, the US government created or reorganized at least 263 organizations to tackle some aspect of the war on terror. The amount of money spent on intelligence rose by 250 percent, to $75 billion (which did not include "black" budgets for classified operations), more than the rest of the world at the time spent put together. A building boom for intelligence agencies meant that the equivalent of three Pentagons' worth of office space was under construction, costing additional billions of dollars. That was in addition to the construction of a new DHS headquarters, the largest government site in half a century.

Zakaria laid out something else I had already noticed during my first year as a cabinet secretary: the government's penchant for churning out undigestible quantities of classified information, some of it far from revelatory. The new apparatus produced 50,000 reports a year—136 a day—few of which were even read or, much less, led to policy change. More than fifty bureaucracies tracked the flow of money to and from terrorist organizations, and by 2010, 30,000 people were employed by the government exclusively to listen in on phone conversations and other communications in the United States. The rise of this national-security state "has entailed a vast expansion in the government's powers that now touches every aspect of American life, even when seemingly unrelated to terrorism," Zakaria wrote. "In the past, the US government has built up for wars, assumed emergency authority, and sometimes abused that power, yet always demobilized after the war. But this is a war without end. When do we declare victory? When do the emergency powers cease?"

Responding to Zakaria's critique, I said I didn't think the homeland security apparatus was overdrawn. I cited the evolution of the kinds of threats and possible tactics in the few years since 9/11. Already in 2010, we saw terrorists moving away from large, complex conspiracies—to smaller, more diverse plots under the guidance of numerous groups that were perhaps inspired by but not limited to only al-Qaeda. I noted IEDs, small arms, and hydrogen peroxide–based explosives designed to be put in backpacks and left around smaller targets in the United States as dangers at the time. The evolving threats meant that we had to constantly reevaluate how best to minimize risk. We needed some planned redundancy—that is, duplication of efforts across agencies at various levels of government—but we could do more to ensure that duplication in the intel area made sense and was not a waste of resources. As always, we have to be able to show that we are spending tax dollars wisely and well.

This imperative for self-evaluation is even more important now. I was taking care in choosing my words at the time because I didn't want to undermine my own department's work, but more than that, I was presenting the facts as they were known at that moment. The government did improve its pre-9/11 capabilities to conduct surveillance and share intelligence, but the threats are continuously evolving, as are the technologies that we and our adversaries use. With the benefit of hindsight, I know it is time to do a soup-to-nuts review of

America's homeland security apparatus. We must ask some fundamental questions: Do we have the right agencies doing this work, and
are they guided by clearly articulated missions? Are people trained
for their jobs? Have we in fact broken down the silos among federal
agencies with overlapping jurisdictions that prevent the right information from getting to the right people? Can state and local partners
get the intelligence they need in time to intercept an attack? By the
same token, can local law-enforcement officials get information up
the chain to the federal government in time to make a difference?

I am not naive enough to believe that such a review would result
in a massive overhaul of how we organize our nation's security. The
federal government doesn't change course on a dime and enact massive organizational change, absent a response to a crisis like World
War II, in the case of the Department of Defense, or 9/11, in the case
of the Department of Homeland Security. But a review like this could
reveal areas for greater organizational efficiency and areas where
greater statutory clarity is needed. It could also provide the American
people with greater confidence in how their government is acting to
protect their safety. And we could flesh out whether Americans have
unnecessarily sacrificed personal liberty and privacy in the name
of enhanced security. I think we will be surprised to see how much
of our personal data is floating around today, not because the government has it but because consumers have willingly shared it with
private companies, whether by uploading fingerprints and financial
information through our smartphones or sharing private behavior
on apps, whether that data reveals a person's preferred pizza top-
pings, dating websites, resting pulse rate, or political views. We give
a lot more away about ourselves than we did in 2001, when concerns
about privacy were more easily dismissed in the name of security.

In the months after the 9/11 attacks, Attorney General John Ashcroft discouraged talk about violating civil liberties in the war on terror with a harsh warning: "To those who scare peace-loving people
with phantoms of lost liberty, my message is this: your tactics only

aid terrorists." Ashcroft reflected an attitude common among policy makers after 9/11 that security and privacy exist on some kind of push-me-pull-you axis. Dial up security, and law-abiding people must be prepared to sacrifice some of their privacy as a result. Work too hard to preserve the privacy of personal data—for instance, to protect images of travelers' bodies taken by airport scanners or their immigration records or fingerprints or, today, to refuse the government's request to open a suspect's iPhone—and we could unwittingly aid those trying to kill us.

I came to government through a career in law enforcement, and I understand this line of thinking. In law enforcement, the impulse is to hoover up as much information as possible to successfully prosecute crimes. Through my experience at DHS, I now understand that security and privacy are not a zero-sum game. At DHS, my chief privacy officer was an attorney named Mary Ellen Callahan, who came to the department from the private sector, where companies were starting to pay greater attention to the privacy implications of customer data. Mary Ellen had a booming voice and the confidence to match it. She was not intimidated as she tried to educate some of her law-enforcement colleagues during internal DHS meetings on the privacy implications of planned surveillance or law-enforcement actions, only to hear the Ashcroft theory that she was "helping the terrorists." She would respond to anyone who challenged her for not being tough enough by imagining a future congressional committee asking what went wrong that allowed another attack. "I have no problem testifying before the next 9/11 Commission, if we need one," she would say. "I'm open to having a talk about how I supported the Constitution."

The question of a trade-off—100 percent privacy or 100 percent security—is outdated, if it ever was the case. The more relevant question is how the privacy analysis is integrated into any security program so that it is taken into account from the outset, a concept known as "privacy by design." For example, when TSA put out a request for bids on a new body-imaging device or full-body scanner, Mary Ellen and her team saw to it that the request-for-proposal specifications included a number of privacy provisions. Bidding companies had to build a system that would not store body images beyond a certain, very limited period for review; place operators in a separate room from those being scanned, in pairs; and prevent any illicit copying of body scan images onto personal devices or USB drives.

Constitutional protections aside, in airports frequented by celebrities, this possibility is not inconsequential. The more privacy-protective approach—to review and analyze generic silhouettes rather than images—was not yet mature when we needed to rapidly launch the advanced imaging technology (AIT) screeners after a failed bombing attempt in 2009, so we implemented those privacy protections. When we first launched AIT, the algorithm kept detecting pants zippers as metal, requiring a pat down every time, which is why we used human screeners initially. But we pushed on the companies to refine their detection algorithms to better identify anomalies. We terminated the contract of the company that could not replace the actual image with the generic silhouette. Now all scanners that TSA operates use the generic silhouette, thanks to our initial privacy requirements and continued pressure.

When the principles of privacy by design are applied, they not only make it easier to uphold people's Fourth Amendment rights against unreasonable search and seizure, they save money and aggravation in the long run. By incorporating clear rules about the capture and storage of personal data at the beginning, it helps reduce the need for big engineering changes or administrative delays when a program involving technology, such as body scanners or other biometric data, is introduced. Mary Ellen also helped DHS figure out how to handle the vast amounts of data on US persons and non-US persons in our various immigration databases and to further slice that information into different tiers of "good guy data" and "bad guy data" and secure it accordingly.

Good guy data concerns passport information, addresses, and financial information, among other things, on legitimate travelers.

Bad guy data might concern ICE lists of people with repeated immigration violations, criminal convictions, and those who have customs violations for smuggling or other crimes. They deserve a closer screening—and have foregone the ability to have significant privacy protections. DHS became adept at quickly getting bad guy data from CBP databases to analysts at the National Counterterrorism Center and others in the intel community, without violating the privacy of the good guy data.

The United States performs a census every ten years. In today's evolving security landscape, a decennial security review, led by a panel of accomplished citizens, comparable to the 9/11 Commission, would be a worthy investment. In the absence of such an overarching effort, we can at least strengthen the work the Department of Homeland Security performs in its quadrennial review. We can ask whether it is successfully performing the work envisioned by Congress.

In 2009, I ordered that all component agencies of the department have a privacy officer directly reporting to the head of the agency, mirroring the successful design Congress mandated by requiring a chief privacy officer for DHS. We should explore what DHS does well and where its performance can improve. We can assess whether the twenty-two agencies combined under one roof at DHS were the right ones or whether some other structure would be more effective.

Those are the operational questions. We also need to ask ourselves some hard questions about the American state of mind nearly two decades after 9/11. Which risks are we willing to accept as a free and open society, and which are we not? For instance, Americans have made the decision to provide easy access to firearms, including civilians purchasing combat weapons. When a psychopath slaughters fifty-eight people and injures more than five hundred firing his legally rigged machine gun from his hotel room into the concert crowd below or a distraught high school dropout opens fire on his classmates, it is classified as a "mass casualty event." We see soul-searching, tut-tutting, and something-must-change laments on television but no meaningful policy outcomes. When a self-proclaimed ISIS sympathizer runs people down on a New York City bicycle path with his rental truck or an immigrant couple mow down their coworkers at a Christmas party or a single shooter does the same at a nightclub, it is called "terrorism." The president might even tweet that the death penalty is called for.

These violent episodes all result in the loss of life; the difference is in the motivation behind the crimes. A mass shooting with no connection to terrorism is investigated by local law enforcement and handled by local prosecutors, with support on an as-needed basis from the feds. Once a possible link to a terrorist group or ideology is identified, however, the feds take the lead, and the entire security apparatus of the federal government comes into play. We can argue whether such a distinction is rational—after all, people still end up dead—but that's the way the system works right now. It is important, though, to understand a perpetrator's motive in order to design and deploy effective prevention strategies in each case.

True security means doing a better job of educating the public about which threats are real or likely and which are not. Cascading natural disasters resulting from the effects of climate change, localized terror attacks (including mass shootings), and ever more brazen and consequential cyberattacks and public health crises are real; undocumented immigrants running over an open border by the millions and attacking Americans in the streets is not. Once the true risks are identified, we can more effectively direct resources to reduce them and get buy-in from the American people.

True security means that as a society we must decide what risks we are willing to tolerate in return for preserving our way of life. Free and open societies require free and open spaces. Imposing an authoritarian lockdown in the name of security, as we had to in the days following the 9/11 attacks, is not who we are as Americans. Nor is a zero tolerance policy at the US-Mexico border, resulting in the appalling spectacle of children being separated by US border agents from their undocumented migrant parents. That failed approach to law enforcement is a waste of our resources, a stain on our international reputation, and a human rights violation. It in no way enhances our security.

True security means less time and resources for endless security theater before Congress and more time on genuine problem-solving. Now that the DHS is in its second decade, it is high time for Congress to streamline its oversight of the department. Accountability is essential, but it must be rational and efficient. More than 100 committees and subcommittees exercise some form of jurisdiction over DHS. The number varies and goes as high as 119 (depending on ad hoc commissions). Even as secretary, I could not have given you the definitive number on any given day.

The department must divert thousands of staff hours from more important tasks to never-ending hearings, requests for briefings, and preparation of (rarely read) reports. Having a cabinet secretary testify is a big deal. It requires hours of preparation, practice sessions, and prehearing briefings with staff to discern what a member is likely to ask in order to provide the department's overseers with the most accurate and thoroughly researched response. Not that all that preparation always paid off. I remember one time testifying before the House Judiciary Committee. Representative Louie Gohmert of Texas, a leader in the Tea Party movement, asked a long, convoluted "question" (about what I do not recall). When I said that I wanted to break my response into two parts, Gohmert thundered, "I don't have time for answers!"

In my five years as secretary, I testified before Congress fifty-five times, and my deputies did so many times more. Between January 2009 and 2014, DHS officials testified at nearly eight hundred congressional hearings and had a total of 10,584 "nonhearing engagements" with

Congress, which include such contacts as meetings and briefings. That number does not include emails exchanged between DHS and congressional staff members and DHS reports prepared at Congress's request. If we threw those in, it would take a big-data analyst to come up with the number. This is more than an annoyance and an inefficiency; it is a threat to our security. Those thousands of staff hours and the focus of the secretary and top leadership can be better directed to operations. The 9/11 Commission recognized this in a follow-up report it issued in 2014, concluding, "This Balkanized system of oversight detracts from the department's mission and has made Americans less safe."

I was called to testify so often that my staff and I eventually made a game out of it. If I made it through a hearing without a significant mistake or deviation from my formal testimony, we got to stop at Shake Shack on the way back from the Capitol to our office. I know that accountability and transparency are essential, but the extent to which I was hauled in front of this committee or that and the time it took away from doing my work was incredibly frustrating.

Congress, of course, has an important oversight function. Americans have the right to know what DHS is doing to make them safer and to know how their tax dollars are being spent. The forward-looking question is, "How do you most effectively and efficiently steer this behemoth called the Department of Homeland Security?" We can answer this while saving a whole lot of time and money if we apply common sense. But the task is beyond DHS. Congress has to reorganize the outdated committee system that has changed little since it authorized the department in 2002. This oversight has led to absolutely numbing levels of redundancy.

It is also time to educate members of Congress and the voters who elect them on the fact that the Department of "Homeland" Security is something of a misnomer. Much of the department's work is international, and DHS has personnel stationed throughout the world. During my tenure, we negotiated agreements with foreign countries on aviation security, information sharing, border security, and port operations, to name but a few. Success requires collaborating with partners, recognizing our shared interests, and accommodating different legal systems—in other words, being diplomatic. Since 2001, the United States has negotiated a series of agreements with the European Union on passenger name records (PNR), which allows US Customs and Border Protection to receive names, itineraries, addresses, and credit card information of incoming passengers, so they can be vetted. Earlier agreements were found to violate EU law, where privacy restrictions are much tighter than in the United States. Once Mary Ellen started playing an integral role in the design of the 2011 agreement, implementing privacy by design in these and other negotiations, later privacy agreements have withstood EU scrutiny.

So much of the work that we do comes from the understanding that if we wait until a threat manifests itself on our shores, we've waited too long. Finding a coherent center for the DHS is the key to better security for the country, and while it was something I worked on, I'll admit that on the day I left office, there was still a long way to go. Yet DHS has made us safer. How much more it can do and how it can meet its challenges are fair and urgent questions.

PART II

WHAT WE GOT RIGHT

CHAPTER 5

Pushing Out the Border

At 9:25 a.m. on September 11, 2001, twenty-two minutes after the second hijacked plane hit the World Trade Center, Federal Aviation Administrator Jane Garvey issued a ground stop over US airspace, forbidding takeoffs and requiring planes in the air to land as soon as safely possible at the nearest airport. The order, implemented for the first time since the invention of aviation in 1903, applied to civilian, military, and law-enforcement aircraft, any one of which could have become a potential weapon on that day. The ground stop affected 36,000 to 40,000 flights that took off daily in the United States in 2001, as well as all general aviation flights. It also banned flights from other countries into the United States, forcing more than 250 aircraft to make unplanned landings in Canada. Altogether, thousands of travelers found themselves stranded in airports and on tarmacs, including a former vice president of the United States, Al Gore. As *Time* magazine wrote, "The FAA had stopped the world."

Amtrak canceled all train service in the northeast corridor from Boston to Washington, and Greyhound suspended bus operations in the Northeast and other parts of the country. The US Coast Guard immediately mobilized more than two thousand reservists in the largest homeland defense operation since World War II and restricted ships at sea from entering US ports. With the increase in security and the grounding of flights, cross-border traffic began to back up, causing delays of up to twelve hours along US land borders with Canada and Mexico. Over the next two days, the lines at the borders stretched from ten miles in Canada and thirty miles in Mexico, as US Border Protection agents opened every trunk and scrutinized every vehicle, person, and piece of cargo entering the United States. I was stunned to learn from Michael Chertoff that in 2001 there were eight thousand forms of identification valid for crossing US land borders—including library cards. Obviously, things are different today.

The response to seal off the United States from the world by land, sea, and air was an understandable defensive measure in the face of unknown danger in that moment. It reflected the same impulse to pull up the ramparts we saw when Congress passed the PATRIOT Act. But the shutdown also serves as a textbook case of how, had it been sustained, it would have destroyed our economy. The economic total impact of the closure of the US borders following 9/11 was $1 trillion. Maintaining the flow of people and goods is essential to our economy and our way of life. Choke it in the name of security and we fail at our mission.

The effects of the border shutdown on 9/11 are a good example of why the Department of Homeland Security was structured the way it was, bringing all agencies securing US land, sea, and air borders under one roof. This mission is why Customs and Border Protection (the nation's largest federal law-enforcement agency), TSA, and the US Coast Guard are all part of DHS. Our system facilitates lawful border crossing by persons through immigration and lawful goods and cargo through customs. We have the US Border Patrol to combat illegal migration between the ports of entry on land and the Coast Guard to do so at sea.

The TSA was created by Congress two months after the 9/11 attacks. First assigned to the Department of Transportation in 2001 and then moved to DHS in 2003, the Transportation Safety Administration replaced the many private firms who operated under contract with single airlines or groups of airlines, using a given terminal, and managed air travel security. TSA was assigned to develop policies to protect US transportation, especially airports, and to prevent hijacking. Setting up the TSA required the largest hiring project in US history—the only effort that compared was processing recruits for the US armed forces during World War I. Between February and December 2002, 1.7 million applicants were assessed for 55,000 positions.

Complaints about TSA are as familiar to me as to anyone, and I know things are far from perfect on the front lines at our airports, even as the agency enters its second decade. During my tenure at the DHS, I constantly heard the horror stories from people at the hands of the TSA. I remember one particularly awful episode involving John McCain, who was instructed to raise his arms above his head during an airport screening. McCain was, of course, badly injured during a plane crash in the Vietnam War and spent years as a prisoner there with two broken arms and was unable to raise his arms above his head. I was mortified.

Of course, the distress cuts both ways. Being a TSA screener is one of the most stressful and thankless government jobs in existence. Turnover at the agency is among the highest within the federal government (right up there with being in President Trump's cabinet), and job satisfaction is ranked the lowest. During my first Thanksgiving in office, I went to work the TSA line at Reagan National Airport in Washington, DC, in part to understand the job that our fifty-five thousand screeners perform each day but also to show that I understood how hard their jobs are. On the Wednesday before Thanksgiving, I donned my blue latex gloves and worked the line, running empty bins from one end of the conveyor belt to the other. Since my official government portrait now hung in every airport, a lot of passengers quickly recognized me. Comments ranged from "What are *you* doing here?" to "Now you see what we have to go through," to, let's just say, less printable observations.

I don't think I have ever seen so many shoes in my life! I left after two hours, thoroughly wrung out and with a renewed appreciation for the pressure my employees were under, relying on technology but also their own eyes to spot something dangerous. TSA agents are the last lines of defense for something getting on a plane, and they often work under brutal conditions. People are rude and aggressive in an environment that is equally unpleasant for the professionals trying to keep them safe. I also left wondering how fast technology would catch up so that people could leave their shoes on and bring their liquids with them on planes. If we had been able to crack that challenge without blowing up the federal budget, maybe I would be president by now!

Few things irritated members of Congress more than the shortcomings of the TSA. And no wonder, given how often they fly and how often they hear complaints from their constituents. We were often asked why the United States couldn't be more like Israel, where security measures include passenger profiling based on appearance and behavior, multiple screenings in the terminal, and checkpoints for all vehicles in the general vicinity of the airport. Consider this: the United States has 450 international airports; Israel has one major international airport and one scheduled to open in 2019. Israel's Ben Gurion Airport processed about twenty million passengers in 2017; TSA handles that many in a week. Lawmakers and airlines have deemed the costs of Israeli-style security measures prohibitive in the United States and would no doubt also object to some of their profiling tactics. Deputy TSA administrator John Halinski was often grilled on Capitol Hill for perceived inconsistencies in TSA procedures. "How come you are doing one thing at this airport and something completely different at another?" a member of Congress would ask. "You shouldn't do that."

Halinski would respond, "Yes, we should. You can look at different security measures depending on the threats. Warm Springs, Idaho, is not as big a threat as JFK."

There has also been a lot of publicity surrounding stress tests run by various undercover TSA "red teams" that resulted in unacceptably high rates of failure to detect harmful items. Some of the criticism is valid, and some is exaggerated—the red teams definitely highlighted weaknesses in our system, but they also often had specialized knowledge designed to trick it.

Nonetheless, considering the 2.6 million screenings that TSA performs *each day*, their batting average is reasonably high—and is improving. It's important not to let the YouTube moments of Grandma getting a pat down or agents inspecting diapers get more attention than the security advances that have been made. It's life-and-death business, but during my tenure, it seemed to be the only department that regularly made it onto late-night television. Now, sadly, many cabinet departments seem to be taking a turn.

One of the major shifts we made during my tenure was to move to a risk-based approach to passenger screening. That is, if we could identify passengers who raised no concerns before they got to a checkpoint, we could allow them to keep on their shoes and jackets and expedite them through the lines. That concept gave rise to TSA Precheck, which is exactly what the name implies—a way to vet a passenger for any known security risks before they get in line. It is easily the most popular thing I've done in three decades of government. More than five million travelers are already taking advantage of the program used at two hundred US airports and by forty-seven airlines. By 2018, 93 percent of TSA Precheck passengers waited less than five minutes to clear a dedicated lane at US airport security. Over Memorial Day weekend of that year, the kickoff of the summer travel season, DHS reported the wait time for 99 percent of these passengers averaged under ten minutes. Not bad, if I may say so myself.

The checkpoint is only one part of a multilayered approach to airport security, which also includes behavior-detection officers, explosive-detection canines, and random testing of luggage and travelers for traces of explosives. Coupled with the arming of cockpit doors and positive baggage matching (ensuring that travelers cannot put luggage on planes and then not board them), the country has effectively ensured that a reprise of a 9/11-style attack cannot happen. But there remains the risk of human error and technological failure. That is why we need the actions of alert passengers, as we saw in the case involving the would-be shoe bomber, Richard Reid, in 2001. This is another example of the importance of having an engaged populace. We need partners, not victims.

Sealing the country on 9/11 also taught another valuable lesson: it is most important to recognize that border protection does not begin at the actual physical borders of the United States. The best protection is prevention, stopping the transit of illicit cargo and persons who intend harm before they ever reach the United States, while at the same time facilitating legitimate travel and trade. This is the principle of pushing out the borders, which is the equivalent of preventative medicine, as opposed to waiting until emergency surgery is necessary. We don't wait to address issues when they happen, but we anticipate and prepare for every distant scenario imaginable.

Homeland Security under my predecessors, Tom Ridge and Michael Chertoff, was an inward enterprise, driven by urgent necessity and trauma after the 9/11 attacks. When I became secretary in 2009, DHS was emerging from start-up mode, and my team and I were able to step back and take a more systematic look at where best to establish our defenses. Pushing out the borders was the principle we extended from the Bush years to better secure the homeland. Another helpful thing about this concept was that it applied just as well to illegal immigration as to terrorism prevention.

When migration from Central America via Mexico into the United States surged in 2014, our assessments showed that many of the threats were not to be found at the US-Mexico border but, rather, much farther south in El Salvador, Guatemala, and Honduras. More than sixty-eight thousand unaccompanied minors from these countries came to the United States, prompting a humanitarian crisis. In the immediate term, we worked with authorities in Mexico to secure their southern border with Guatemala. That way, we established a first line of defense to stem the migrant flow from countries that did not even share a border with the United States. I told President Obama that our DHS enforcement dollars could be spent much more effectively if other government agencies invested more in diplomatic and economic efforts to address such push factors as gang violence, drug wars, and the weakness of civil institutions, like an independent judiciary.

In 2015, Obama asked Congress for $1 billion to support such efforts in El Salvador, Honduras, and Guatemala; he received $750 million of that request in 2016. Vice President Joe Biden managed the US response to the migration crisis from Central America, which promoted community policing, the establishment of more transparent court systems, and economic rules and regulations to promote investment and reduce the unemployment that feeds crime. US aid also went to youth centers similar to Boys and Girls Clubs, to help young people feel they had a future in their own countries. American aid was linked to measurable progress. By the end of the Obama administration, the murder rate in Honduras was down by 11 percent, Guatemala adopted anticorruption measures, and El Salvador disrupted the financial networks of criminal syndicates.

During the 2014 surge, we saw that our law enforcement did not deter further illegal flows, and neither did other forms of deterrence. The White House even started a public awareness campaign on radio stations in the region, featuring President Obama's domestic policy advisor Cecilia Muñoz cautioning parents, in Spanish, not to send their children to the United States on such a dangerous journey alone. It was not uncommon for the children, once they entered the United States, to seek out a federal Border Patrol agent. From a position of safety, they would claim asylum status and be able to remain in the country, often in the care of a relative, while their cases were processed. We had some limited, miserable experiences with family detention during the Obama administration and shut it down as quickly as possible. In 2016, an ICE advisory committee concluded that DHS "should generally exercise its authority to release family members, together as a family, as soon as possible." This humanitarian approach was a far cry from the Trump administration's family separation chaos in 2018. It was hard enough during the Obama years to care for unaccompanied minors who came on their own. It was unconscionable to cause children to become unaccompanied minors by removing them from their parents.

While political rhetoric is focused on illegal immigration and stopping terrorists at our land borders, arrest data show that the more common risks to homeland security come from other forms of transnational crimes. Human trafficking, drug smuggling, gun running, and money laundering are having more adverse effects at our land borders than terrorism. That doesn't mean that we don't pay attention to terrorism—our central mission—but that we put it in context and in proportion to the existing threats. We have to look at all the flows that result from globalization—the people, goods, ideas, capital, and electrons going north and south across the border—and adjust our policies to reduce them.

We increased the flow of intelligence between the United States and Mexico to better track and stem threats as far south as possible. A major contributor to this early in the Obama administration was the Merida Initiative, a security cooperation agreement with Mexico and the countries of Central America, with the declared purpose of combating drug traffickers, transnational organized crime, and money laundering. The initiative included assistance with training, equipment, and intelligence. Congress appropriated $2.5 billion from 2008 through 2015, a relatively modest investment that produced strong returns. At DHS, we stepped up our efforts with the Mexican federal government to improve our joint capability to seize large drug loads before they got to the border and to find and arrest the traffickers responsible for them.

One example of US-Mexico cooperation involved the arrest, capture, and then recapture of Mexican drug lord Joaquín "El Chapo" Guzmán. The largest exporter of cocaine and other drugs to the United States, El Chapo was the violent head of the Sinaloa cartel. The United States and Mexico exchanged intelligence about his operations and whereabouts for years until he was apprehended (after his second prison escape) in 2016 and extradited to New York, where, at this writing, he awaits trial.

In addition to cooperating with the government of Mexico, we substantially fortified operations on our side of the border. These efforts included a layered approach involving increased manpower between the ports of entry, greater use of sensors and other detection technologies, air cover, and border patrol checkpoints designed to apprehend people and loads before they reached the interior of the United States. By the end of the Obama administration, illegal border crossings were at a forty-year low.

There is still much to do—going forward, we need to have an integrated, strategic plan including the State Department, DHS, and the Department of Justice to work with the governments in those countries to improve the quality of their own homeland security. This means strengthening their law-enforcement capabilities and their civil institutions, such as justice systems, to contain gang violence. We have many examples of successful gang-eradication strategies that have worked in the United States. Strategies can include prevention, intervention, and suppression. While gangs remain a problem in some US cities, the problem is far reduced from what it was in the 1990s. We ought to share and support similar efforts in these countries.

We want our Border Patrol agents to have what is referred to in law enforcement as "domain awareness," but we have to keep the likelihood and severity of the threats in perspective. A border designed to stop crime and criminals of all sorts is going to be better equipped to deal with terrorists than one focused solely on controlling undocumented immigrants. It is counterproductive and inaccurate to insist, as President Trump has, that the US-Mexico border is a popular gateway with terrorists.

As I learned painfully on Christmas Day during my first year in office, when a twenty-three-year-old man was caught trying to ignite explosives he had smuggled in his underwear aboard a US-bound flight, if the problem is at your border, you've got, well, a problem. The passenger made it through six international airports on his way to the United States carrying explosives. As a result of what we learned from that failure, we expanded an existing program to screen passengers at last-point-of-departure airports before they fly to the United States. Through a series of agreements with host governments, we increased the number of US Customs and Border Protection agents stationed at high-risk airports overseas. If a CBP officer received derogatory information about a passenger planning to board a US-bound flight, he or she could ask the host country security agent or airline to prevent the passenger from boarding or even remove the passenger from a flight before it departed. We also started requiring that data about travelers of interest be shared forty-eight hours in advance of their departure to the United States. This gave our agents more time to request additional vetting or prevent the passenger from boarding.

We also expanded a customs preclearance program to conduct full security checks, including immigration and customs, on foreign soil. Preclearance had been around for years but was used primarily as a convenience to expedite the passage of US-bound travelers from certain countries. For example, US military personnel flying through Shannon, Ireland, or travelers coming in from Canada could be screened at their departure airport abroad rather than getting in line to be screened once they landed in the United States. In the context of counterterrorism, I saw that preclearance was a remarkable security tool for the United States and a valuable economic tool for foreign airports and carriers. It meant that our CBP officers would be screening passengers abroad, so we knew the work was to our standards and quality. For international partners, expedited passage through US Customs at their airports added convenience for travelers, which is a great way to win business. President Obama saw the benefits too and readily agreed when I proposed expanding preclearance into other countries.

It was not always easy to establish a foothold. One of our first partners was a Middle Eastern ally, where we ran into a dispute with our hosts over whether our US officers would be allowed to carry weapons in their countries. Our allies were not thrilled by the prospect of armed American agents in a potential shootout in their airport. We finally compromised by agreeing to store our agents' firearms in a locker, with keys held by both the US and the host country's agents. I'm glad to report we haven't had to use them yet.

At other times, disrupting standard procedure took some pushing—and being seen as pushy. In 2009, we were in Copenhagen, pushing out our borders by negotiating for armed Federal Air Marshals to board US-bound planes from Danish airports. The justice minister told us to see the transportation minister, and he, in turn, sent us to the interior minister. Each Danish minister was tall and handsome, with chiseled features and perfect English. I tolerated the game for a bit, but my team and I soon grew frustrated with the rope-a-dope. "I've got an idea," I responded during one session. "How about we shut down all air traffic from Denmark into the United States while we think about this?"

One of the Danish ministers got the point. "Madam Secretary, that's a very American way of doing things," he said in clipped English. But a few days later, Federal Air Marshals began working the skies over Denmark. Crisis averted, at least that time.

In addition to posting CBP officers in foreign airports, we took other steps to push out US borders: sending customs inspectors abroad to inspect US-bound cargo containers, increasing the number of Homeland Security attachés at US embassies, and increasing the role of Immigration and Customs Enforcement (ICE) in our visa programs. Just as the Department of Defense is still evolving seventy years after its creation at the end of World War II, I expect that the Department of Homeland Security will do so as well, in response to changing threats and technologies.

We gave a significant boost to the responsibilities of the US Coast Guard. More than any other military branch, the Coast Guard has a reputation for having to do more with less—over its 228-year history, the Coast Guard has been assigned to the Departments of the Treasury, US Navy, Transportation, and, since 2003, DHS. The Coast Guard has eleven missions, from search and rescue to fishing inspection, with a fleet of ships more than 40 years old, about forty thousand active-duty personnel, and a budget of just above $10 billion. That's about 6 percent of the US Navy budget for the same time period. Since 9/11, the Coast Guard has become the primary defender of ports, water-ways, bays, and 88,633-mile shoreline of the United States, responsi-ble for container security as well as border security. Despite its many missions, few Americans know what the low-profile Coast Guard does. In 2016, the agency removed some $6 billion worth of illegal narcotics from vessels in US waters, saved more than 5,000 lives, and screened 32.4 million merchant vessel crew members and passengers as potential security threats prior to arrival in US ports.

The Coast Guard is there in times of emergency, responding to natural disasters, such as Hurricane Katrina in 2005 and Hurricanes Harvey, Irma, and Maria in 2017, as well as environmental disasters, such as the massive BP oil spill in the Gulf of Mexico in 2010. One aspect of their job that is little known or appreciated is that they are tasked with protecting US interests in the Arctic. That requires a fleet of ice cutters, which are tremendously expensive vessels. When I arrived, we had a fleet of exactly two ice cutters, one of which was in long-term dry dock for extensive repairs. Indeed, most of the Coast Guard fleet was aged to an embarrassing degree. The conditions for the crew were especially harsh, with berthing areas that lacked space for the increasing number of women serving on board. We needed to add separate quarters for them. Because the Coast Guard budget comes from DHS, however, and not from the Department of Defense, we continually scavenged for the resources necessary for them to fulfill their mission. After the severe hurricane season of 2017, the Coast Guard received increased funding to fix damage to its vessels and facilities and reduce its extreme maintenance backlog. Continuing to boost funding for the small but mighty Coast Guard will be dollars well spent in advancing our homeland security.

Customs, Border Protection, TSA, and the Coast Guard are each unique functions within the federal government. Though there may be some joint operations or intelligence sharing, especially with the FBI and the DEA, no other entity has the central mission of land, air, and sea protection. Pushing the borders out means expanding the international reach and presence of these agencies. As secretary of *homeland* security, I learned that the work is inherently transnational and that international partnerships are key. I traveled to forty countries during my years in office, establishing strong relationships with my counterparts abroad, typically the interior minister or home secretary, and persuading them to buy into our policy of pushing out the borders. Aside from a few hiccups, such as those I described above, most of my counterparts found it mutually beneficial to intercept risks before they reached US borders.

In 2010, a sharp-eyed British customs agent disrupted a plot to bomb US-bound aircraft using bombs secreted in printer toner. The agent received actionable intel about a printer in a shipment originating from Yemen, for which someone had paid $500 in shipping fees on cargo worth only $100. Closer examination revealed that the printer contained the components of a small but powerful bomb that was traced to al-Qaeda in the Arabian Peninsula (AQAP), an organization whose explosive handiwork was becoming well known to us.

The United States now works to intercept suspicious travelers and cargo before they reach US borders or airports. Of course, pushing out the borders does not account for threats that emerge from cyberspace or those that arise domestically within the United States from homegrown terror organizations or lone wolves. I will address these in later chapters. But by expanding its reach internationally, the Department of Homeland Security has increased the country's ability to keep us safer. Greater incorporation of DHS into US foreign policy objectives and strategies would more fully recognize DHS's role in creating a safer country at home and, by extension, greater safety around the world.

The growing isolationism of the Trump administration is at odds with the global nature of homeland security. We need to rely on other nations to enhance our security, as they need to rely on us. Cooperation agreements to help identify and intercept suspect travelers and cargo are essential in our growing homeland security toolbox. I can only imagine how difficult it is for our agents on the ground in foreign countries when the president is trumpeting his "America First" policies. In a world of global terrorism networks, international cooperation matters. Going it alone makes us less secure, not more.

CHAPTER 6

Shrinking the Haystack

Throughout much of my law-enforcement career, the tools of security were guns, gates, and guards. The theory was that we protect important places by keeping out the bad guys and run them down if they break through or try to escape. Prevention and prosecution of crimes were enabled by intelligence that came from two primary sources. One is humans, or HUMINT, for example from spies, informants, law enforcement, or foreign governments. The other is signals, or SIGINT, coming from wiretaps, digital communications (including financial transactions and other sources), and, of course, video surveillance. Once, when I was a US Attorney in Arizona, we actually hid a camera behind the terrarium in a white paramilitary gang clubhouse. As my prosecutors and I watched the surveillance video of our suspects, we'd watch snakes slither in front of the camera lens, sometimes obstructing our view. You'll be happy to know we ultimately prosecuted members of the (aptly named) Viper Militia for a variety of weapons and explosives charges and secured ten guilty pleas and two convictions.

Today, guns are still guns, but our other tools have changed dramatically. Happily, I haven't had to watch a snake video in decades. Our most important "gates" are less visible than people realize and are built from such advanced technologies as biometrics and surveillance devices, including drones, radio frequency identification tags, sensors, and, yes, the dreaded body scanners at our airports. Our "guards" rely on intelligence increasingly gathered through big data, meaning the collection, storage, and analysis of enormous quantities of information in search of patterns and anomalies that help law enforcement. In this area, especially, we have made remarkable improvements over the systems we had in use on September 11, 2001.

We've been able to do this in part because the period since 9/11 coincides with an explosive growth in digital technology that has transformed big data in three key areas known as the "three Vs": volume, variety, and velocity. We track more information from a wider number of sources that pours in at ever higher rates of speed. As the cabinet secretary dubbed "Big Sis" by right-wing media, I can confirm that the Department of Homeland Security is getting better at collecting and managing data that identifies people and things posing a threat to the United States. We were far from perfect, but we were pretty damn good. There is also a fourth "V": veracity. We tried to have greater confidence in the accuracy and security of the data we analyze, although that's a difficult standard to achieve in the current environment.

The members of Congress who oversee the DHS budget visit the National Targeting Center for Cargo and Persons (NTC), but their constituents know little about it. I think they should. It will help them feel safer. The NTC is a large, tan building in a Virginia suburb of Washington, DC, not far from Dulles International Airport. It was created two months after 9/11 and has grown so much it had to be moved to its new location in 2017. The NTC is the crown jewel of the American homeland security operation, consisting of two large command rooms flanked by a ring of offices where every person, plane, vehicle, vessel, and piece of cargo entering the borders of the United States is tracked in real time.

A row of giant wall-mounted TV screens and clocks of the world's time zones gives the large open spaces the atmosphere of mission control. Dozens of Customs and Border Protection agents, along with others from the TSA, FBI, Drug Enforcement Administration, US Department of Agriculture, Customs, the Coast Guard, and others, study screens that are refreshed constantly. FDA agents read data from radiation sensors to detect the presence of a bioterrorism agent on an incoming plane, vehicle, vessel, or container. Intelligence and border agents from key US allies work there too, combing through data in other languages and from their own nations' intelligence services. Whether agents are tracking a terrorist or a tourist smuggling a prosciutto ham, it is literally on the radar at the NTC.

Border Protection officers look at passenger manifests and compare names and aliases with biometric and biographic data about each person of interest. Fake passports are exposed through mismatched fingerprints, iris scans, DNA samples, and other tricks of the trade. A traveler's biographic data will tell us not only what nationality the person is (or claims to be) but where that traveler has been prior to booking a flight into the United States and, in some cases, whom they have been in contact with abroad.

Travel ban authors take note: it is not the nationality of the passenger or the passenger's last point of departure into the United States that is most relevant but the traveler's airport of origin plus itinerary, matched with a lot of other data, that tells us someone is a potential bad actor. A passenger who has visited a country identified by the United States as a State Sponsor of Terrorism, or who may have been to other countries known to harbor terrorist groups on a previous itinerary, is of great interest to us. That much is true. But that is not enough. Few terrorists are so dumb as to come directly from or travel on a passport of a country known to harbor terrorists. We watch travel patterns that bring passengers from dangerous countries into the United States on routes that hopscotch through perfectly respectable airports in Europe, Asia, Africa, the Middle East, and Latin America. The patterns change constantly, and we watch for those changes too.

None of this is as sexy as a wall. It's not as satisfying. There are no photo ops and no mythology, because few people know the National Targeting Center even exists. But this is what true Homeland Security looks like. The NTC makes one billion data transactions in a twenty-four-hour period, each equivalent to matching a piece of data to a traveler or a piece of cargo. Put another way, the NTC captures data in quantities that sound like they are borrowed from science fiction: exabytes and zettabytes and even yottabytes (named after Yoda from *Star Wars*). All the information in the US academic research libraries takes up two petabytes. All words ever spoken by human beings measure five exabytes. The NTC houses one of the largest data-collection programs in human history, in quantities exponentially larger than we have gathered data before. It provides the Department of Homeland Security with the real-time, 360-degree view of all US borders that was lacking on 9/11.

The National Targeting Center houses the new approaches to the homeland security mission, and it represents a remarkable improvement over the systems in use on September 11, 2001. Imagine the NTC as a series of concentric rings that start securing the US homeland far from our land borders, in distant air and sea ports, and continue until the last point of defense, where a traveler or piece of cargo actually arrives in the United States.

Perhaps most importantly, we have shifted to risk-based analysis of potential threats. A US citizen who has traveled, for example, to Yemen, Somalia, or any other country of interest may be of far greater interest to DHS than a Yemeni or Somali national who is traveling to the United States for reasons that may not be detrimental. It depends on what the intelligence shows us at any given time, not what politicians want to hear. The key concept is to reduce or derisk. And to effectively derisk, it takes reliable information. When dealing with massive amounts of data needed to protect the borders of a country as large as the United States, we need the right algorithms to analyze data about passengers and cargo.

My border security adviser, Alan Bersin, likened our challenge to a modern twist to the age-old question: what's the best way to find a needle in a haystack? One is to burn the haystack down, in a sense capitulating to terrorists. This would be the equivalent of sealing off the border, as the United States did on 9/11, and bringing lawful travel and trade to a halt. The second is to look at every piece of straw. That was the approach in the days after 9/11, when the border was still effectively shut down, and the lines of vehicles stretched ten miles north into Canada and three times as far into Mexico, as agents opened every trunk and suitcase and looked at every person. It became quickly clear that this would have delivered to al-Qaeda the victory that it sought in terms of destroying the modern economy. The third method is to get specific information so that granulated intelligence permits us to reach into the haystack and find the needle, because we know where it is. While intelligence has gotten a lot better, it's not a foolproof way to find the needle.

That leaves us with the fourth method: shrinking the haystack. The idea is to apply the doctrine and strategy of risk-based assessment to the data to expedite the movement of low-risk individuals and cargo, so finding the needle is a less daunting search. By expediting lawful trade and travel, we can in fact increase the security profile, because it means that the haystack is so much smaller. Since 98 percent of all travel and trade across US borders is perfectly lawful, we look for the needle in the much smaller haystack comprised of the 2 percent of trade and travel that is possibly illicit and dangerous. DHS expedites the flow of people and goods known to be low risk so that we can focus our resources instead on those persons or cargo about whom we have derogatory information or lack sufficient information to make a judgment about the degree of risk they present. That's a critical principle of DHS, and the National Targeting Center is where DHS manages the data and makes the risk assessments that underpin the department's work. In 2011, I instructed TSA to develop a way to expedite travelers and goods that we have enough information about to classify as low risk. This approach led to our most effective and popular trusted traveler program, TSA Precheck. Global Entry, which is operated by US Customs and Border Protection, runs on the same principle and allows US citizens returning from abroad to receive expedited screening when they get to a US airport.

The idea is to collect personal data, make a judgment that the vetted travelers are low risk, and expedite their movement across the border or through an airport so that we can focus on those who may pose threats or about whom too little is known to make that determination. In exchange for data that permits DHS to vet people and for the promise that we will maintain that information about them in confidence and use it only for the purpose for which they give it, the traveler is allowed to travel through US airports without having to remove their shoes and belts or take laptop computers out of their cases (although they still may not carry more than four ounces of liquids). The application process can be started online, and an in-person background check must also be conducted. Travelers who are foreign citizens must meet certain residency requirements to qualify for the program.

DHS algorithms give agents the ability to do real-time checks on a real-time basis, for every person and every piece of cargo crossing into the country. We can compare every traveler both biometrically and biographically against databases that indicate people of high risk. The big-data strategy permits us to identify high-risk persons and high-risk goods that pose a threat if they cross into the homeland, while at the same time facilitating the flow of low-risk people and goods necessary for our economy to function. DHS can permanently derisk someone, for example, by enrolling them in TSA Precheck.

Following the same principle, US Customs and Border Protection offers Global Entry, allowing expedited clearance for preapproved, low-risk travelers when they arrive in the United States. Travelers enter through automatic kiosks at select airports where they present their machine-readable passport or US permanent resident card, place their fingerprints on the scanner for verification of identity, and complete a customs declaration. The kiosk issues the traveler a transaction receipt and directs the traveler to baggage claim and the exit. All applicants for the Global Entry program undergo a rigorous background check and in-person interview before they are approved. The Department of Homeland Security operates other federal programs, NEXUS and SENTRI, for verifying the identities of trusted, pre-screened travelers traveling from Canada and Mexico, respectively, to and from the United States. And the Trusted Trader Program, introduced in 2014, provides a system for expediting cargo into the United States through inspected and secure global supply chains. I carefully monitored the waiting time for trucks at the borders and saw them decrease steadily from 2009 to 2013.

As the cost of data storage continues to drop due to advances in technology, shrinking the haystack through data analysis becomes relatively inexpensive and provides significant value in terms of return on investment. By 2022, expenditures on big-data analysis by the Department of Homeland Security and other US public safety organizations is expected to reach $11 billion, according to the Homeland Security Research Corporation. While the world becomes increasingly digital and more connected, we see both threats and opportunities emerging in the homeland security enterprise. The threats are carried on the internet and by other forms of digital communication, allowing bad actors to connect and radicalize, whether they actually organize plots or instead provide ideological inspiration to lone wolves.

The opportunities in the areas of law enforcement result from the explosion of digital data and our ability to collect and analyze it using big-data analytics. This boosts the capabilities of intelligence and law-enforcement agencies in many relevant areas, including counterterrorism, cybersecurity, financial systems and other critical infrastructure, public safety, and managing disasters. Smartphones, wearables, and other connected smart devices, such as GPS, give the good guys surveillance abilities that never existed before.

The case of Faisal Shahzad, the Times Square bomber, is illustrative. On May 1, 2010, Shahzad abandoned an explosive-laden Nissan Pathfinder, set to go off at the height of Broadway theater-going traffic. Some alert street vendors spied smoke escaping the vehicle and informed an NYPD mounted officer, who quickly called in the bomb squad. Once the area was cordoned off, the Pathfinder was detonated, and then the hunt was on for the bomber. By May 3, investigators used all the tools at their disposal, including video surveillance, cell phone tracking, and travel records to identify Shahzad as a person of interest. Significantly, Shahzad had been listed on a US government travel watch list since 1999, because he had been bringing large amounts of cash into the United States.

Despite this, Shahzad had already boarded a Dubai-bound Emirates flight when an alert Customs and Border Protection officer noticed that his red-flagged name was on the passenger manifest. The plane was returned to the gate moments before takeoff, and Shahzad was arrested without incident. Shahzad's case demonstrates how the greater availability of intel facilitated by greater use of technology can accelerate our ability to identify perpetrators. Yet one cannot overvalue the importance of someone doing their job and staying alert.

Another case involved sharing classified information collected on the battlefield with the NTC and with US Citizenship and Immigration Services, when the agency vets people seeking to travel to the United States or obtain immigration benefits. In 2011, the FBI arrested two Iraqi refugees living in Bowling Green, Kentucky, after a sting operation in which they engaged in a plan to send weapons and money from the United States to al-Qaeda. The men's fingerprints were found on parts of an IED used against US troops in Iraq and were entered into a military database. That bad guy data was then shared with the USCIS, which was able to match the identity of the men who had applied for refugee status in Kentucky. The men were arrested and pled guilty in federal court. One was sentenced to life in prison and the other to forty years.

The case became briefly famous when one of President Trump's advisors cited the "Bowling Green massacre" as evidence of the potential danger of terrorists posing as refugees. There was in fact no massacre, but the case did reveal gaps in our refugee screening program, which have since been fixed. The discovery of these two men prompted DHS to make temporary changes to the way Iraqi refugees and visa applicants were admitted into the United States. As a result of their arrests, DHS revetted fifty-eight thousand refugees already in the country, imposed vetting on twenty-five thousand other Iraqi citizens still in Iraq, and tightened the processing of visa applications by Iraqi refugees for six months. The story is relevant not because of the imagined massacre but because of the effective use of data analysis to connect the men's actions in Iraq to their actions in the United States.

Big data allows us to look at patterns and more accurately predict and intercept future threats. We have come a long way since September 11, 2001, in terms of technology and experience. I am confident we are on the right track in shrinking the haystack and making the US homeland more secure. What we need to guard for now is the profusion of data being created and captured, which is increasing exponentially. The gobs of information generated by smart devices—such as GPS trackers, Fitbits, home speakers, smartphone apps, and so on—not to mention what people disclose on social media, invite intrusions into individual privacy. They also add a whole lot of hay to the stack, for law-enforcement and intelligence agencies trying to sort out what is relevant to public safety and what is not.

CHAPTER 7

Zigging and Zagging

One of my favorite events as governor of Arizona was joining my Mexican counterpart for his annual *cabalgata*, an elaborate two-day horseback ride in the Mexican border state of Sonora. One year, dressed in denim and a cowboy hat, with a huge Mexican flag flying from a pole attached to his saddle, Governor Eduardo Bours Castelo led three thousand riders from the Livestock Association of Sonora through the rugged scrub country and across the Cumpas Mountains south of the Arizona border. I am not much of a rider, so Governor Bours saw to it that I had a horse that was gentle but fast enough to keep up with his white stallion at the head of the cavalcade. Bours took his responsibilities as host seriously and pointed to the law-enforcement helicopters that sometimes flew over the cabalgata as a sign of his commitment to my safety, even as he dismissed media reports about cartel violence in the region. He also made sure that my staff and I had a comfortable motor home to sleep in at our campsite—and that it was stocked with copious amounts of beer and tequila, which everyone enjoyed after a long day of riding.

The ritual was important not so much for policy reasons but because we were neighbors. As governors, Bours and I recognized that regardless of the differences between our countries' governments, the citizens of our respective states were bound by a common economy, culture, and physical environment. Whether we were dealing with adverse weather conditions, the price of beef, illicit drug traffic, immigration, or even tips for boosting tourist spending, Eduardo and I thought nothing of calling each other directly, rather than routing formal communications through the US State Department or the Foreign Ministry of Mexico. Our staffs were likewise friendly and shared information and advice as well.

Governor Bours and I were both committed to good relations between Arizona and Sonora, and we made an effort to attend regular meetings of the Arizona-Mexico Commission, which alternated between our two states. Our personal participation led to the growth and importance of these meetings. By the time I left the governorship, they were attended by hundreds of business leaders, educators, and health professionals from both sides of the border, divided into committees and jointly working on projects of shared interest. We wrapped things up with great parties and lots of music and dancing at dinner on the final night. What was important was seeing citizens from both countries tackling thorny issues—from fast lanes to expedite the movement of cargo across the border, to the environmental conditions at the Colorado River, to improving children's health—together. In private conversations, Eduardo and I shared our misgivings about our respective federal governments. At the time, the policies of President George W. Bush and Mexican president Vicente Fox, whether on border security or trade, seemed at times removed from conditions Eduardo and I experienced on the ground in Arizona and Sonora.

These strong personal connections are at the heart of my approach to our relationship with Mexico. From my childhood in Albuquerque to my work as US Attorney and then attorney general and governor of Arizona, my experience on the ground gave me a deep understanding of the rich heritage and complexity of our ties—and of the value of two neighbors chatting over the "backyard fence" as Eduardo and I had done for years. In fact, while I was governor of Arizona, I spent more time working with the governor of Sonora than I did with many of my US counterparts. I struggled with how easily this human factor was erased from political arguments I got tangled up in as secretary of homeland security.

Whether in testimony before Congress, discussions made at the White House, white papers from think tanks, or during shouting matches on cable television, the debate was all too often dogmatic, predictable, and unproductive—frozen in time. We have long had bipartisan consensus that the US immigration system is broken but can gain no traction on fixing it. Eleven million undocumented people now live in the shadows, unwilling to report a crime, cooperate with law enforcement, go to a shelter in times of disaster, or even venture out to have their children vaccinated. This compromises the security of our communities. In the corner of my office at DHS, I kept a beautifully tooled black leather western saddle, a gift from Eduardo after our final cabalgata. As I sat there late at night listening to talking heads on CNN or FOX or MSNBC in the background spouting border theory, while I pored over another futile draft of the next day's testimony or talking points for a cabinet meeting, I thought often of those days in the saddle and just shook my head.

The US border with Mexico stretches 1,954 miles from the Pacific Ocean to the Gulf of Mexico and is one of the longest land borders in the world. It is also the world's most heavily trafficked land border. Each year, 350 million people, five million cars and trucks, and $44 billion worth of freight cross legally at forty-eight ports of entry located in California, Arizona, New Mexico, and Texas. Most of border country, though, is rural. First surveyed in 1849 and amended numerous times since then, the US-Mexico border snakes along an arbitrary line drawn by nineteenth-century surveyors through the deserts of Chihuahua and Sonora and then shifts at the Texas border along the deepest point of the Rio Grande until it empties into the Gulf of Mexico.

Portions of the borderlands are so bleak and inhospitable that William H. Emory, the US Army engineer who surveyed the Texas side of the border in 1844, described it to his superiors back in Washington, DC, in stark terms. "Imagination cannot picture a more dreary, sterile country," Emory wrote. "The very stones look like the scoriae of a furnace." Francisco Cantú, a former US Border Patrol agent, wrote a memoir of his experiences in the desolate Tucson sector, which included all too often retrieving the corpses of migrants who had succumbed to the elements in the desert.

Few Americans realize that 98 percent of border traffic is legal activity, leaving potentially only 2 percent that is not. Although the border traverses vast tracts of uninhabitable land, it also goes through major cities, including San Diego, Nogales, El Paso, Laredo, and Brownsville, and this is where much of the legal activity between the United States and Mexico takes place. Mexico is our second-largest trading partner. We are their largest. It is the other 2 percent of border traffic that makes the news. Although you would not know it from the headlines, the number of illegal border crossings has steadily decreased over the past decade, reaching a forty-year-low during the final years of the Obama administration.

This is not to suggest that the amount of illegal traffic is acceptable. It is not, both from a law-enforcement and a humanitarian perspective. Each year, an average of four hundred people die in the desert or the mountains between the United States and Mexico, from heatstroke or dehydration, drowning in the Rio Grande, or suffocating in locked vehicles and cargo containers after being abandoned by panicked smugglers. US Border Patrol agents pick up the decomposing corpses and bring them to the nearest morgues to be returned to Mexico. They take injured and ill survivors to local hospitals and the able-bodied to local detention facilities, until Immigrations and Customs Enforcement (ICE) agents can collect them and begin the deportation process.

Increasingly, our Border Patrol agents find hungry and terrified children as young as six, with no adult nearby. They bring the kids to a detention facility, where they are held for a short time until they can be reunited with a family member. Sometimes the children must remain overnight in cells fitted with adult-sized beds. Most of the children are not from Mexico but rather from Central American countries, and the younger ones are often found dehydrated and dazed, with no idea of how they ended up at the US border, unable to provide even basic information, such as their name, hometown, or date of birth or who they are looking for in the United States. If no relative can be found, as is often the case, the children are taken by the Department of Health and Human Services to be placed in foster care until their case can be resolved. The problem became so widespread that at DHS I heard about Border Patrol agents spending their own money to keep stashes of candy bars and coloring books at their stations.

In the ignorance and confusion that so often shapes our media coverage of the border, these children were often misidentified as Mexican, contributing to the misperception that Mexicans were "flooding" over the US border. They were not. Border apprehensions of Mexican nationals went down 85 percent during the Obama years. By 2017, 57 percent of border apprehensions were classified as "OTM," or "other than Mexican."

The human face of this migration finally pierced the public's consciousness during the Trump administration's zero tolerance fiasco that resulted in thousands of family separations in 2018. The pictures and audio of traumatized children being held in border detention centers awaiting transportation to foster care and of toddlers being forced to sit in court to be addressed by a judge were sickening. After the public revolted, President Trump signed an executive order purporting to keep families together, while still insisting on his zero tolerance policy. This put CBP, and by extension DHS, in a terrible position, as the Justice Department had neither the facilities to detain families together nor the resources to swiftly prosecute the adults and resolve their cases.

The 2018 crisis was the most dramatic to date but by no means the only one on our southern border. The disconnect between the debate about the border and what actually happens at the border is one of the most vexing problems I faced as secretary of homeland security. The border is the big stage when it comes to security theater, a venue that most Americans know little about. Try as I might, I could not break through with the facts. Most of the news and nearly all the mythology is generated by the 2 percent of the human and cargo traffic that is illegal. Through personal experience, I know that pathos and tragedy are more often the story than are the cartoon tales told by politicians of terrorists, machete-wielding rapists, gun runners, and gang members, or "professional mountain climbers," in Donald Trump's words, evoking an image of people catapulting over a rickety fence while a US border guard snoozes against a nearby cactus.

During a visit to the San Diego side of the border in 2017, Trump told reporters: "As horrible as it sounds, when they throw the large sacks of drugs over, and if you have people on the other side of the wall, you don't see them—they hit you on the head with 60 pounds of stuff? It's over." I can't even imagine where this story came from, and the fact that the president could make such a claim and not be challenged on the spot speaks to the confusion and lack of firsthand knowledge so many Americans have about our border with Mexico. Yes, drug smuggling has long been a problem, and US authorities work very hard, regardless of which party is in power, as do our Mexican counterparts, to stop that traffic and arrest and prosecute the perpetrators. For the record, narcotics traffickers tend to build elaborate tunnels to smuggle drugs, or they hide drugs in vehicles crossing through ports of entry; they do not fling them over existing border fences and walls, in some fictitious version of the drug-smuggling Olympics.

Unlike many in Washington, I know this border. I've walked it, flown it by helicopter, and of course, ridden it on horseback. I've been in the drug tunnels where cocaine and marijuana by the ton come into our country and the sewers where children who are crossing the border alone sleep at night. I've seen the campsites strewn with abandoned clothing, human waste, and refuse. I also supervised the prosecution of more than six thousand immigration felonies, plus dozens more large-scale drug-trafficking and money-laundering rings. I have seized assets and sought to convert them into something more useful, including a domestic violence shelter in Douglas, on the Arizona side of the border. Other needs abound. In Tucson, for example, we expanded the morgue, in part due to the number of migrants who die in the rough, rugged Arizona desert country, carrying only a plastic water jug.

I've also been at the crossroads of the toxic political debate for a long time. As a US Attorney, I supervised the prosecution of repeat illegal immigrants and the smugglers who make their lives a misery. As governor, I vetoed bills from my legislature aimed at curbing illegal flows, because I deemed them harsh and ineffective, for instance mandating workplace raids that round up low-wage earners rather than going after the employers who create the demand for illegal workers in the first place.

At other times, it would appear I was on the side of the hardliners. During the George W. Bush administration, I declared a state of emergency and was the first governor in the nation to call for the National Guard at the border, when illegal border crossings surged through my state as the result of poorly coordinated federal operations that clamped down on illegal traffic in California and Texas, in essence funneling migrants through Arizona. Yet I also refuse to agree that a wall by itself is an answer. As I told anyone who would listen, "You show me a fifty-foot wall; I'll show you a fifty-one-foot ladder."

And I was not above a little security theater myself to make my point. When the Bush administration tightened enforcement in California and Texas in 2006, we saw an alarming rise in the number of undocumented migrants coming across in Arizona, an estimated four thousand a day. Taxpayers have valid complaints. I get it. In Arizona in those years, emergency rooms near the border filled to capacity, sometimes beyond, with undocumented immigrants who were literally dropped off around the corner by US Border Patrol agents, so the federal government would not have to foot the bill for their care.

With the border sealed in other sectors, Arizona became a funnel for coyotes, as smugglers are known, and the prices for their services soared. The black market for stolen cars used to transport undocumented migrants multiplied, as did the market for fraudulent documents that are used to get jobs illegally. Our criminal justice system was especially hard-hit. If an undocumented immigrant commits a crime in Arizona, that person is typically not given bail. He or she spends more time in jail than most prisoners and is indigent, as a result getting representation from a public defender, paid for by the Arizona taxpayers. If convicted, the foreign national is sent to a prison system that has more inmates than beds, forcing the Arizona Department of Corrections to resort to triple bunking and lock-up beds. During the Bush years, the number of foreign nationals in Arizona jails and prisons grew by 60 percent.

As a governor, I did not have the luxury available to the US Congress of running a deficit by printing more money. I had to balance my budget each year. Ever the stickler, I decided to bill the Bush administration under a federal program intended to reimburse states for the incarceration costs of illegal immigrants. So I sent President Bush's attorney general, Alberto Gonzales, an invoice. When I got no response, I sent another and then another—seven in all. The first one was for $77 million, and the last one, including late fees, totaled $357 million. We made a blow-up replica of the invoice and held a press event at the state capitol, gleefully attended by politicians of both parties. For what hardworking Arizonans absorbed in these costs alone, I told the media, we could have paid for all-day kindergarten for every five-year-old in the state. I scolded the Bush administration and Congress for saying they were against new taxes and yet, by their inaction, imposing an illegal immigration tax on Arizona taxpayers and on the taxpayers of every border state.

Not surprisingly, a check never found its way from the White House to my office in Phoenix. So we took action on our own, beginning with the principal of prevention. First, we set up a statewide task force on fraudulent IDs, the lifeblood of the human smuggling trade. I put in charge the director of the State Liquor Department, who knew a thing or two about fake IDs. Under her direction, the task force disrupted several major fraudulent ID manufacturers, resulting in more than a hundred arrests in eighteen months. We also applied new technologies. I directed Arizona's highway patrol to station mobile cameras on southbound traffic lanes to Mexico and with advanced license-plate-reading technology, we vastly improved our ability to detect the stolen vehicles favored by human smugglers, leading to arrests of the drivers. We took commonsense law-enforcement practices and worked with our Mexican partners to ensure that our police radios, used by both states, interconnected. My friend Governor Bours ordered checkpoints in Sonora to be established, and on my side of the border, we deployed additional Arizona State Police.

We took this combination of law enforcement and humanitarian measures on our own, punishing the perpetrators of human smuggling while dealing as compassionately as we could with their victims, even those technically in violation of US law. This is what I mean by zigging and zagging. I refuse to concede that illegal immigration is a political winner for those who simplistically suggest we simply seal the border with a wall. I won reelection as governor with 63 percent of the vote, carrying every county and legislative district in my state, despite the fact that my opponent's chief complaint against me was that I was somehow soft on immigration. I'm not and never was. He lost.

As governor, I would meet periodically with Senator John McCain, usually at his office in north Phoenix, and no matter what the designated topic, our discussions always came around to immigration and the border. He was clearly unhappy with the management of the Tucson sector, which at the time was the most heavily trafficked sector along the southwest border, and I was concerned as well, because the flood of traffic along that corridor was injecting a flood of antiimmigrant fervor into Arizona politics that I had not seen before. And even people I saw as moderate in their views were very angry and frustrated and insistent that we do something.

At the time, in 2007, Congress was struggling to take up comprehensive immigration reform, and Jon Huntsman, then the Republican governor of Utah, and I assembled all the governors of the western states, from both parties, some very conservative, some very liberal, to agree to an immigration reform proposal that bore all of our signatures. When I presented it to McCain at his office in DC, I saw a rare flash of the temper he was famous for. "This doesn't help me," he said, as he threw the signed proposal down and said it didn't go far enough. I was surprised, because I thought our efforts showed you could reach a bipartisan consensus that goes a long way toward a solution. I said that the governors wanted to be helpful and wanted Congress to act. He was annoyed that the governors had not taken on one of the thorniest issues, which was a path to legal status for the eleven million undocumented immigrants already living in the United States. I share McCain's frustration over the inability of Congress to get immigration reform passed. And I wonder whether, as an institution, it is capable of dealing with one of our country's most difficult challenges. But rooting the debate in fact rather than fiction would at least be a start.

We need the courage to talk honestly with the American people about immigration, and we must have federal legislation that is reality based. The popular notion that we deport all eleven million undocumented people to their country of origin and then invite them to apply to get back in the United States is a joke. That presumes at a minimum that we have the administrative and legal infrastructure to handle such a mass exodus. We don't. Eleven million people—that's like asking everyone who lives in New York City and Los Angeles to get up and move. So let's turn to reality.

Here are the key elements of a real border plan: The first is the development of innovative, technology-driven border control between the ports of entry. Boots on the ground definitely help, but we can shore up our border gaps with ground-based sensors, radar, and unmanned aerial vehicles for wide-area intrusive detection. Any combination of the above will work far better than any wall, tall or short, "beautiful" or not. The Department of Homeland Security installed this kind of technology during the Bush and Obama years and needs continued funding to sustain their efforts, as technology evolves. Second, we must fundamentally reform the visa system and streamline the visa process. I agree with the majority of Americans that we have a problem, though I do not agree with President Trump's solution to cut the types and numbers of visas granted. Our current system doesn't make sense. For example, the Dominican Republic has a population of about eight million people. The Republic of Mexico has about one hundred million people. Yet under the current visa system, the Dominican Republic per capita is allocated more visas than Mexico. No wonder it takes on average more than ten years to get a legal immigrant visa from Mexico. Few can afford that kind of patience.

We need to widen the legal labor pool and match the evolving labor needs of the United States. Hiring needs fluctuate in many areas, including agriculture, hospitality, construction, technology, engineering, and nursing, to name but a few. We need to make it easier for people with the needed skills and educational qualifications to come in legally to meet demand, so as to remove the incentive to be in the country illegally. This means increasing the number of visas we award, not reducing those numbers, as some in Washington currently suggest.

While we're at it, we need tamper-proof immigration documents to quell the fraudulent ID market. By adjusting our visa processes, we can end the backlogs at the same time as we meet the rapidly changing demands of our agricultural, bio, and high-tech industries. Third, we must institute a temporary worker program. Foreign labor should not be a substitute for US workers, but it is critical that we bring foreign workers out of the shadows, put the clamps on the underground labor market, and bring greater stability to our workforce.

We also have to acknowledge that illegal immigration is a supply and demand problem and that Congress must address both sides of that equation. Employers who hire illegal immigrants and know it should be held accountable and penalized. There are existing federal verification systems for employers, but they're not enough. Those systems need to be able to interface with Social Security databases, so employers can perform real-time verification that actually means something. We have the technology. We need to put it to work. Employers who defy the law and feed the demand side of the illegal immigration equation should be punished. This means providing additional resources to the Department of Justice for employer enforcement and prosecution. I made this argument as governor of Arizona. I made it as secretary of homeland security. It is galling that I am still making it a decade after I started.

Finally, we must continue to modernize our border infrastructure and strengthen border enforcement. Over three successive administrations since 1994, in a completely nonpartisan way, starting with Operation Gatekeeper in the Clinton administration and continuing with the investments made by George Bush and Barack Obama, we have been making continuous improvements. The United States has increased the number of federal Border Patrol agents from three thousand in the 1990s to twenty-two thousand today, with nearly nineteen thousand on the US-Mexico border. Additional investments in aircraft, intelligence, and reconnaissance capacity in terms of sensors and airborne surveillance have made the border safer than it has been in decades. Physical barriers may provide visual and psychological comfort to politicians on the US side, but Americans need to understand that border security is increasingly provided by air-craft, drones, and sensors, not by an agent with night-vision goggles and a lasso.

Immigration enforcement is an area ripe for shrinking the hay-stack. On my watch at DHS, we ended workplace raids and other all-encompassing round-ups that some think look good on TV but aren't actually very effective. Instead we focused on the deportations of criminals, although we had continued difficulty sorting out the millions who committed no crime since arriving in the United States, including those who arrived as children, from those who posed a danger to public safety.

It was that desire to separate those who posed a threat from those who did not that led to my proposal to the president in 2012 that we defer immigration enforcement action against those who were brought to the United States as children, allowing us to instead direct our limited enforcement resources to actually improving public safety. There was also an important economic argument: it is a waste of human capital to deport educated taxpayers or future taxpayers and a waste of limited enforcement resources to hunt down and deport law-abiding young people known as Dreamers, whose only "crime" was being carried across the border as infants or young chil-dren, instead of focusing on criminals and border crime posing an actual threat to public safety.

In the absence of action from Congress to help these young people by passing the DREAM Act, President Obama was looking for exec-utive action. He asked me for a plan. I directed my staff to come up with a system to identify and protect the estimated 1.8 million young people who were brought to the United States as children. Our first draft was strong but had a typically DHS-style name: "Exercising Prosecutorial Discretion with Respect to Individuals Who Came to the United States as Children." Ouch. But once we changed the name to the Deferred Action for Childhood Arrivals—or DACA—we were off and running. The creation of DACA reflected my beliefs that our nation's immigration laws must be enforced in a firm and sensible manner, but they are not designed to be applied blindly. Nor are they intended to remove productive young people and ship them to countries where they may not have lived or even speak the language. Our plan allowed those eligible to register for protection from deportation by Immigration and Customs Enforcement. As long as recipients remained enrolled as students or employed or enlisted in US military service and did not commit any crime, they would receive a renewable two-year deferment of any enforcement action, as well as a work permit.

President Obama announced Deferred Action for Childhood Arrivals on June 15, 2012, the thirtieth anniversary of the US Supreme Court decision barring the government from charging illegal immigrant schoolchildren tuition. "These are young people who study in our schools, they play in our neighborhoods, they're friends with our kids, they pledge allegiance to our flag," Obama said in a speech in the White House Rose Garden.

> They are Americans in their heart, in their minds, in every single way but one: on paper. They were brought to this country by their parents—sometimes even as infants—and often have no idea that they're undocumented until they apply for a job or a driver's license, or a college scholarship. Put yourself in their shoes. Imagine you've done everything right your entire life—studied hard, worked hard, maybe even graduated at the top of your class—only to suddenly face the threat of deportation to a country that you know nothing about, with a language that you may not even speak.

Despite the introduction of DACA, the zigging and zagging continued. We had proven our humanitarian and economic credibility through DACA. "This is not a path to citizenship. It's not a permanent fix," Obama said. "This is a temporary stopgap measure that lets us focus our resources wisely while giving a degree of relief and hope to talented, driven, patriotic young people." In other words, a zig. It was no substitute for comprehensive immigration reform, which would address the backlog of all eleven million undocumented residents in the United States. In an attempt to get Republicans in Congress back to the negotiating table, Obama continued to enhance his border security efforts. A zag.

Deportations continued apace, leading to harsh criticism from the immigrant rights community. President Obama was deeply wounded when Janet Murguía, the National Council of La Raza president, said at the group's annual awards dinner in 2014 that Obama would be known as "deporter in chief." Obama said the next day that he wanted to reduce the effect on families as a result of the broken immigration system, ordering my successor, DHS Secretary Jeh Johnson, to review deportation policies. A few months later, Obama said he would shield as many as five million undocumented immigrants from deportation and allow many of them to work in the United States legally.

Speaking to the American people in 2014, the president hit many of the important notes I wish circumstances had permitted us to make earlier. Noting that deporting millions is not who we are as a nation, Obama addressed those "living in the shadows" and the communities they supported. "Are we a nation that tolerates the hypocrisy of a system where workers who pick our fruit and make our beds never have a chance to get right with the law?" he asked. "Whether our forebears were strangers who crossed the Atlantic, or the Pacific, or the Rio Grande, we are here only because this country welcomed them in." Today, millions still living in the shadows are looking for evidence of his words. And the world is watching how we treat them.

CHAPTER 8

"The System Worked"

On Christmas Day, 2009, my brother and I went for our annual postbrunch walk in the woods near his home in Danville, California, about thirty miles east of San Francisco. When we returned, the Secret Service agent who was traveling with me was waiting in the driveway. As soon as I heard, "Ma'am, you are needed on the secure line," I knew the news would not be good. I was directed to the backseat of my government van to call John Brennan, President Obama's top counterterrorism advisor, who was at the White House while the president vacationed in Hawaii. Brennan was brief: a young male passenger on a flight from Amsterdam to Detroit that afternoon had been subdued in the air while trying to ignite explosives laced into his underwear. At first I thought I hadn't heard correctly. In his underwear? The true identity of the man, traveling on a Nigerian passport, was not verified. We did not know who, if anyone, was directing the operation or whether there were more such "underwear bombers" aboard flights headed to the United States that Friday, as the holiday week began. "Janet, you need to run this down," Brennan said, instructing me to find out whether other bombers were en route.

As soon as Brennan and I hung up, I immediately contacted my chief of staff, Noah Kroloff, and had him convene a classified NICCL

(National Incident Communications Conference Line) call. At DHS, this meant senior officials, including the heads of the TSA, Customs and Border Protection, the Secret Service, and our Intelligence and Analysis Division, as well as others throughout government. While my family sat down to Christmas dinner, I perched in the guest room upstairs, rounding up my senior staff and top aviation, customs, and intelligence officials across the US government. The key players were scattered, trying to enjoy a rare day off with their families after a grueling first year in office. Noah was in Phoenix; my deputy chief of staff, Amy Shlossman, was in Washington, DC; my counterterrorism advisor, Rand Beers, was traveling outside of the Capitol region; and my communications head, Sean Smith, was in Oregon. Noah also rounded up acting CBP commissioner Jayson Ahern and acting TSA head Gale Rossides. Within a half hour, six key members of my team were on the NICCL call, racing to get answers to Brennan's questions—and most importantly, to take all necessary steps to apprehend any other would-be bombers headed for the United States.

We quickly reviewed the facts known at that hour. Umar Farouk Abdulmutallab, a twenty-three-year-old citizen of Nigeria, started his journey three days earlier in Yemen. He then flew to Ethiopia and Ghana and finally Nigeria, where he embarked on his failed bombing mission. He was able to fly from Lagos to Amsterdam and there board a plane bound for Detroit with a small packet of plastic explosives—PETN and TATP—sewn into the crotch of his underwear. Shortly before landing, he tried to detonate the explosives by injecting them with a syringe filled with liquid acid. That's when passengers and crew noticed the odor and tackled him. Abdulmutallab was badly burned in the process. While we were getting more intel about the would-be bomber, we quickly moved to deploy enhanced security measures at all airports worldwide serving as last points of departure to the United States. We also put out an alert to all air crews flying into the United States and began combing again through all the passenger manifests of all US-bound aircraft to see if anyone in transit raised a red flag. Even though predeparture screening is standard protocol, we had to eliminate the possibility we had missed someone else.

Within a very short time, it became clear that there were enough red flags in Abdulmutallab's story to run a slalom race. He began his five-country odyssey in Yemen, number one on the US list of "countries of interest" with known links to terrorists. He paid $2,831 in cash for a round-trip ticket from Lagos to Detroit via Amsterdam. Even though he did not trip a classic terrorist indicator, a one-way ticket, the cash purchase was unorthodox in a number of ways and should have triggered further security screening. Despite being on a US terrorism database of more than half a million people, Abdulmutallab was not on shorter lists of people banned from flying into the United States or automatically subject to additional screening. (The larger list of 550,000 can include people who might have minor customs infractions and so is, in and of itself, not a reliable predictor of violent threats.)

We would later learn that only five weeks before the failed attack, Abdulmutallab's father, a prominent Nigerian banker, had reported his suspicions that his son was involved with Islamic extremists. The tips were duly recorded at the US embassy in Abuja but were not forwarded to all relevant agencies in the States and seem to have been shelved as a result, since they did not trigger a response. We also learned that Abdulmutallab had showed up on a British watch list, when he filed fraudulent information on a visa application. For reasons unknown, a recent National Security Agency report about a Nigerian believed to be working with al-Qaeda in Yemen did not trigger a cross-reference to a list of Nigerian citizens, including Abdulmutallab, in the terror database maintained by the National Targeting Center. There had been a massive screw-up.

Abdulmutallab was in custody in Detroit and speaking freely to the FBI interrogators from his hospital bed at the University of Michigan burn unit. He confessed that he had received his explosives and instructions in Yemen from a bomb maker affiliated with al-Qaeda in the Arabian Peninsula (AQAP). AQAP, formed early in 2009 through a merger of the Saudi and Yemeni branches of bin Laden's terror organization, had in a short time become its most lethal division. Abdulmutallab was connected at the highest levels. He said he had received spiritual guidance while in Yemen from Anwar al-Awlaki, the radical US-born Muslim cleric known as the "bin Laden of the internet." Among al-Awlaki's pupils were three of the 9/11 hijackers, as well as Nidal Malik Hasan, the US Army psychiatrist who had opened fire in November 2009 at his fellow soldiers in Fort Hood, Texas, killing thirteen and injuring thirty.

How had a passenger about whom we had so much information boarded a flight bound for the United States without triggering any enhanced screening? And how many more such travelers had we missed? If there was scarce comfort to be taken from the torrent of fresh intelligence, it was that Abdulmutallab reported his botched attempt was not part of a wider wave of attacks. The US intel community reported no human or signals intelligence to indicate Abdulmutallab was lying.

Not wanting to take the suspect entirely at his word, I ordered TSA to put a stop on all 128 flights coming into the United States for several hours, while we cross-checked passenger manifests against databases of known and suspected terrorists, as well as more restrictive no-fly lists. Within four hours, we issued new and draconian vetting measures for passengers boarding planes into the United States. Before we allowed air traffic to resume to the United States that afternoon, we insisted that transit countries agree to our procedures, effective within hours, prompting some tense and most un-Christmas like conversations with our allies overseas. One senior TSA official reported that when he called his German counterpart at home to convey the new requirements, requiring the dispatch of additional German airport police overnight, "I thought he was going to choke me through the phone."

Late that afternoon, I got on a secure conference line with members of President Obama's national-security team. They reported that the president, vacationing in Hawaii, had been read in on the intel and was understandably not happy. He wanted to know how Abdulmutallab had managed to get through so many traps and come within moments of causing the largest aviation catastrophe since 9/11. Like everyone else, he wanted to know how Abdulmutallab got on that US-bound plane, in fact on six planes over three days, with explosives in his underwear. We did not have satisfactory answers, and we knew it. We at least knew the answer to the most urgent question: was he part of a wider conspiracy? The suspect's confession was consistent with new reports from US intelligence and that of our allies. Abdulmutallab was not part of a wider conspiracy. We reported that the threat was contained.

With millions of Americans scheduled to fly home from their Christmas vacations in the coming days, the president wanted to assure the rattled public that they were safe to travel. I was quickly booked on the Sunday morning talk shows to deliver the message and thirty-six hours later, I drove across the Bay Bridge into San Francisco at 3:00 a.m. Pacific time, to make the programs live on the East Coast. I spoke to each of the network anchors by "two-way remote," meaning that the interviewer sat in a studio in Washington, DC, while I appeared on a split screen from San Francisco. Each time I was asked if it was safe to fly, I responded with variations of the message that US and international aviation authorities had the situation well in hand and that Americans could rest assured as they boarded their holiday flights home.

There must have been a split screen in my brain as well. I wanted viewers to understand that there was not an airborne squadron of underwear bombers headed for the United States. US and international aviation authorities had been working around the clock since Christmas Day to comb the intelligence, examine flight manifests, and enhance screening worldwide to make sure that was not the case.

"I think the important thing to recognize here is that once this incident occurred, everything happened that should have," I told Jake Tapper, then the anchor of ABC's *This Week*. "The passengers reacted correctly; the crew reacted correctly; within ninety minutes, all 128 flights in the air had been notified. And those flights had already taken mitigation measures on the off chance that there was somebody else also flying with some sort of destructive intent." I was holding my own until I made it to the last interview of the morning, with CNN's Candy Crowley, and in my exhaustion telescoped the message into three unfortunate words I hope will not end up chiseled on my tombstone: "The system worked."

Of course, the system hadn't worked. I knew that. Everyone knew that. Later that Sunday, I flew back to DC aboard the DHS secretary's specially equipped Gulfstream jet, operated by the Coast Guard. The five-hour flight was a blur of piecing together intelligence and secure phone calls. By the time I landed, all hell was breaking loose over my comment. I saw Representative Peter King, a New York Republican who was chairman of the House Homeland Security Committee, call for my resignation on TV. I was further dismayed to see the president have to clean up my blunder, when he went on television from Honolulu to acknowledge the obvious. "A systematic failure has occurred and I consider that totally unacceptable."

When Obama returned from Hawaii after New Year's Day and convened the national-security team in the Situation Room, he listened impatiently as Brennan, CIA director Leon Panetta, Michael Leiter (head of the National Counterterrorism Center), and I briefed him on developments. Obama was not prone to emoting, but the president's displeasure was evident, and he did not mince words. He barreled through the dots we had failed to connect. "I want these things fixed, and I will hold you accountable—you, this group around the table, accountable for fixing that process and that is where my focus is going to be, not on who messed up." Although I felt terrible, I was prepared. Before the meeting, I asked to meet with the president in the Oval Office. He listened quietly, grinding his jaw muscles, as I apologized for the grief my comment had caused him. I later realized his purpose had not been to take me to the woodshed but to give me a private moment to unburden myself and to let me know I still had his confidence. "We all make mistakes, Janet," Obama responded with characteristic graciousness. "I'm counting on you to help us come up with a better system."

Finally, I paid a visit to Representative King, explaining my mistake and all that we were doing to correct the missteps that the Abdulmutallab episode revealed. I believe when you make a mistake, it is important to acknowledge it and fix it. Congressman King and I developed a good working relationship after that, and we went on to coordinate closely on later events like the federal response to Hurricane Sandy, which devastated his district in New York and many others in 2012. Perhaps it seemed obvious then that relationships matter, but in our current political environment, it bears remembering.

While the events leading up to the failed mission of the underwear bomber went down in the headlines as perhaps our most embarrassing failure, I am confident that what we did in its aftermath will be recorded in the longer term as one of our most significant successes. The Christmas Day plot was a huge eye-opener. One, it showed that notwithstanding all the work that had been put into intelligence sharing between the intel community, our foreign partners, and law enforcement since 9/11, there were still dangerous gaps. In particular, there were gaps in getting intelligence from our national-security agencies into the hands of Customs and Border Protection and others who are responsible for assessing who is getting on a plane and flying to the United States. There were also coordination problems with the Department of Justice, whose agents administered the Miranda warning to the suspect advising him of his right to remain silent before DHS agents had finished their interrogations. There is a public safety exception to the Miranda warning intended for exactly such cases, and we worked with our colleagues at Justice to clarify our mutual understanding of this exception.

The second revelation was that there were bomb makers out there who were constantly developing new threats. While we were busy studying the past, they were studying how to attack in the future. We were focused on securing airplanes coming into the United States, while they were developing bombs that could circumvent that same security. Throughout my time at DHS, we worked hard to change our relationship with the intelligence community and the FBI so that they were more willing to share intelligence with us about what bomb makers were thinking. What were they looking at? What were they learning about our security protocols? And how specifically were they seeking to construct devices to get past security? Bomb making had come a long way since the infamous bungled "shoe bomb" attack in December 2001, when a British citizen and al-Qaeda conspirator named Richard Reid tried to ignite plastic explosives concealed in the heel of his sneakers while on a flight from Paris to Miami.

We became aware of plots that involved surgically implanting a bomb in a terrorist posing as a passenger. The chief bomb maker for AQAP, a Saudi citizen named Ibrahim Hassan Tali al-Asiri who lived in Yemen, seemed to have a fascination for the nether regions of the human body. In February 2009, ten months before the failed under-wear bomb, al-Asiri used the same type of plastic explosive to rig up a small liquid pouch. He then instructed his own brother to insert the pouch in his rectum before he was scheduled to meet with Saudi Arabia's deputy minister of the interior, a Saudi prince who had once ordered al-Asiri arrested. As soon as the brother entered the prince's office in Jeddah and was standing next to him, he blew himself to bits, but his intended royal victim lived. US analysts did not know what to make of the body cavity bomb at the time. Now we were able to connect the incidents.

In response, we brought together our Office of Health Affairs, CBP, TSA, and others from our Research and Analysis Office to discuss what somebody who had a bomb surgically implanted might look like if they came to the airport, what indications of surgery would be visible to screeners, whether there would be a scar, and what other symptoms a person carrying an implanted bomb might show. We set up a protocol so that travel screeners were trained to look for these signs, and if a passenger was exhibiting any of them, we were prepared to quickly move doctors or other medically trained personnel in the airport to assess the risk. Our agents did not come across any surgically implanted IEDs, but the United States did connect the intelligence to more of al-Asiri's handiwork.

In 2010, Brennan received a tip that AQAP was plotting to blow up cargo planes bound for the United States. This time, the explosives were hidden in shipments of printer cartridges. Brennan's source even provided the tracking numbers of the two packages inbound to London on a UPS plane from Yemen. British customs officers were alerted and intercepted the boxes at a freight airport outside of London, well before they were transferred onto a plane to their intended destination, Chicago. As a result of the printer cartridge plot, we completely revamped how we screened and vetted cargo coming into the United States. If we couldn't reliably identify and vet the shipper, we had other screening methods to find explosives or potential biohazards in US-bound cargo. As a result of that effort, by 2010, 83 percent of air cargo was fully screened and vetted prior to being loaded on a US-bound flight. That's a much bigger number than before and a direct result of our strategy of pushing back the borders. Today that number is closer to 100 percent.

As a result of these changes, the Department of Homeland Security started to grow up and became more integrated into the government's national-security structure. As my counterterrorism coordinator, John Cohen, noted, we stopped walking into interagency meetings with the adolescent attitude that "DHS is here, we got this," and started to look instead at the areas where we could add value to an already immense intelligence operation. Instead of DHS trying to recreate what the FBI did or recreate what the CIA did, we focused on leveraging information from the intelligence community with information we were getting from our component agencies, such as Customs and Border Protection, TSA, and the Secret Service, as well as what we were hearing from our partners in state and local law enforcement. For example, local law-enforcement officials from Hennepin, Minnesota, provided information about local Somali youth to help us to better understand how young people were becoming radicalized and recruited by overseas terrorist groups like al-Shabaab. It was information from these same officials that alerted the federal government that young Somalis were beginning to travel from Minnesota, where they were part of a refugee resettlement program, to Syria, where they were joining al-Qaeda–related groups there.

DHS has such broad responsibilities and collects so much disparate information that we provide added value in a different way to our nation's security posture. We could identify a suspect cargo shipment, a passenger for whom there was derogatory info who was beginning to travel, or detections of cyberinfiltrations into critical infrastructure on a real-time basis. That kind of information empowered the government to act proactively to prevent, intercept, and quickly remediate security-related problems.

We saw the benefits of this approach in the aftermath of the 2013 Boston Marathon bombing, which killed three and injured more than two hundred. As tragic as the incident was, it was far less deadly than it might have been. Months before the attack, DHS and local law enforcement and first responders in Boston had conducted a simulated tabletop exercise involving a mass casualty event in the heart of the city. The emergency protocol put in place that day came directly from that exercise. As a result of our performance, DHS had demonstrated its capabilities to leaders from other agencies and showed how we proactively anticipate scenarios that can become all too real. When I first became secretary, I sometimes wondered if the other cabinet heads understood what DHS was there for and why it was so huge and seemed unwieldy. Things changed after the Boston bombing.

And it was time to make that shift. The terrorists' capabilities were constantly evolving, and so were ours. The 9/11 attacks involved a massive, centrally coordinated plot to train and direct terrorists to breach cockpits and turn civilian aircraft into guided missiles. When we hardened cockpits after 9/11, terrorists shifted their focus to getting less-well-trained "mules" to smuggle bombs into the passenger cabins or cargo holds of US-bound aircraft, where they could be detonated over US airspace. None succeeded. This was Terrorism 1.0, the analog model. Each plot required a mastermind, a bomb maker, one or several foot soldiers, varying degrees of training, the transfer of explosives, and international travel involving a short list of countries, false documents, and financing.

Each step of the process was traceable—and at least to some degree, able to be disrupted, in that we were able to correctly analyze intelligence. (As we have seen, that sadly was not always a given.) We also had an understanding of the terrorists' playbook and some degree of predictability, in the form of databases of known and suspected terrorists and their associates—most often, their financiers. We had phone records and intercepts, credit card payments, bank transfers, and digital correspondence. In the first decade after 9/11, the US government got better at disrupting plots using predictive intelligence rather than having to resort to forensic reconstructions of crimes that had already taken place. Yet as we adjusted our security, they adjusted the design of their bombs. Terrorists began using nonmetallic components and different chemicals that would not be detected through our increasingly stringent screening processes. We always had to be one step ahead. We had to know what they were thinking about, what technologies they were studying, and extrapolate what they were trying to design. That part of the 9/11 Commission recommendations we got right.

What we began to see during my tenure at DHS was the emergence of Terrorism 2.0, the internet model. Political ideology and inspiration come not from a mastermind like Osama bin Laden or one of his surviving (and aging) lieutenants or from rivals within ISIS but instead in the form of online videos and seductive tweets designed to lure recruits onto the dark web, where their browsing history and any traceable information about their location disappears. DIY terrorism content is downloadable, diffuse, and free. It requires little to no training, only the will to kill—and to die.

There are other shifts as well. Today's social media jihadists identify with the Islamic State, the former offshoot of al-Qaeda in Iraq, which over the years became its bitter enemy as the result of generational, theological, and strategic feuds with bin Laden's old guard. The faction rebranded itself the Islamic State in Syria (ISIS) in 2013, after that country disintegrated into civil war. While the 9/11 terrorists were highly educated and middle class, today's ISIS-inspired content is designed to appeal to young people who are psychologically fragile or unstable and in search of belonging, connection, and purpose.

In 2007, a New York Police Department study identified three stages such a person goes through in becoming a terrorist inspired by radical Islamic ideology. The first is a personal crisis, such as a failure at school, the loss of a job, a romantic breakup, or the death of someone close. There is typically a political aspect as well, often involving the perception of Muslims being unjustly harmed throughout the world. The second is a "cognitive opening," leading a secular or barely observant individual to adopt fundamentalist ideology and to isolate himself (and it is "he" in almost every case) from those who do not share his views, including family members and clergy. The third is "jihadization," the point at which a person decides to mobilize and commit an act of violence. Would-be terrorists will often at this stage seek out training and financing abroad before striking those they consider "nonbelievers."

In his book *The United States of Jihad*, written almost a decade after the NYPD study, the journalist Peter Bergen details several chilling cases of suburban American youth who succumbed to ISIS ideology and notes some changes. While the personal crisis or alienation phase is often still the starting point of a terrorist's journey, today's recruits are often politically naive, even ignorant, and may not even identify as Muslim. As a result, the cognitive opening may not lead to any observable behaviors, such as adopting conservative Muslim dress and grooming, becoming alienated from family, or switching places of worship, all steps that could alert a family member or clergy person that something is amiss.

Jihadization, or more accurately "radicalization," takes place in the blackest box of all: the human mind. There is no travel involved; no one needs a passport, a bank account, or a coconspirator. Those who self-radicalize tend not to have criminal records. Predictive analytics are almost useless, since these people are not listed in terrorist databases or even in the immense DHS data "lakes" that seek patterns from vast amounts of travel, financial, and communications records. The time between radicalization and action may be days or even hours, leaving a very short trail of clues.

Each lone wolf terrorist is different. Some cases involve a mashup of all the indicators. In June 2016, American-born Omar Mateen, a failed prison guard who later flunked out of Florida State Trooper training, opened fire in the Pulse gay nightclub in Orlando, Florida, killing fifty people and injuring fifty-eight, making it for a brief time the deadliest mass shooting in US history. Shortly after his shooting spree began, Mateen made a 911 call saying that the Boston Marathon bombers were his "homeboys" and declaring his loyalty to ISIS. (Neither of the brothers who perpetrated the Boston attack, both of whom immigrated as children from the central Asian country of Kyrgyzstan, had known connections to ISIS, although one brother did claim to learn bomb making from an online magazine posted by the same al-Qaeda network that armed the underwear bomber.)

Investigators found that Mateen, in the hours before his attack, had made several posts on various Facebook accounts, vowing revenge for US airstrikes in Iraq and Syria. Although investigators later pieced together many political statements Mateen made in support of Muslims over the years and others supporting violence against those who harmed Muslims, Mateen did not appear to lead a devout lifestyle. Reports indicated he drank alcohol heavily, abused steroids, and concealed his sexual behavior with men during both of his marriages to women.

The homeland security challenge going forward is Terrorism 3.0—combating the threats originating within our own borders from a variety of ideologies, whether radical Islam, the right wing, or from mass murderers like the Las Vegas shooter or the Parkland High School killer in Florida, who do not appear to be ideologically motivated at all. The Terrorism 1.0 threats came primarily from abroad during the immediate post-9/11 era. Under the Bush administration, DHS emphasized screening travelers coming into the United States based on their country of origin, who fit the known patterns of terrorism at the time. In addition to understandable concerns about racial profiling and potential civil rights violations, this practice led to excessively large data sets, sweeping up lots of people who had no connection to terrorism. There were violations of our values, yes, but from an operational standpoint, this overly broad approach wasted resources and led to our later strategy during the Obama administration of shrinking the haystack. We moved away from country-of-origin-based profiling to a fully intelligence-driven, data-driven screening and vetting protocol, which has become highly efficient. As we saw in the previous chapter, that principle is equally applicable in securing our border with Mexico.

But during the Obama administration, we too were accused of racial profiling. After the Abdulmutallab scare, we created new rules requiring that citizens of Afghanistan, Algeria, Cuba, Lebanon, Libya, Iran, Iraq, Nigeria, Pakistan, Saudi Arabia, Somalia, Sudan, Syria, and Yemen must receive a pat down and extra security check of their carry-on baggage before boarding any flight to the United States. The new rules were fairly criticized by human rights and civil liberties advocates and, given how predictable they were, were not effective from an operational standpoint. Any terrorist worth his salt would not travel on a passport from one of the countries on the short list.

In recognition of the homegrown Terrorism 2.0 threat, in 2014, DHS under my successor, Jeh Johnson, expanded a program we started called Countering Violent Extremism (CVE). Although designed to ferret out extremists of any nature, whether white supremacists or Islamic radicals, the bulk of the $10 million in annual grants went largely to pilot programs in Muslim and Arab American communities, including those in Detroit, Minneapolis, and Los Angeles, between 2014 and 2016. The department enlisted local leaders, such as teachers and others who worked with young people, clergy, and local law enforcement to communicate with DHS officials in an effort to intervene with those suspected of becoming self-radicalized online. After all, we reasoned, concerned parents and teachers would be more comfortable discussing their concerns with a trusted imam or youth counselor from their own community than with a federal agent. Who wants to turn in their own child?

What well-meaning policy makers failed to understand was that in many cases, violent extremists were not coming from Arab American or Muslim communities. Investigators found that many of the young people we intervened with were ideologically ignorant. Having one of our agents sit down with an imam and having that imam explain to the would-be terrorist why what they were doing wasn't found in the Koran or was inconsistent with the teachings of Islam didn't matter, because they often didn't know anything about Islam. Countering Violent Extremism was viewed in many American Muslim communities—which have been the target of extensive surveillance by law enforcement since the 9/11 attacks, including under the guise of community outreach programs—as just another intelligence-gathering exercise. The program was also handicapped by the lack of reliable metrics for success. How do you measure things that don't happen?

After leaving DHS, my advisor John Cohen conducted a study that found ideology, religion, and ethnicity proved to be less relevant indicators of becoming a terrorist than the vulnerable or peculiar psychology of individuals in search of something to connect with that would make them feel valuable or significant. A $400,000 grant from the Obama administration to a nonprofit group called Life After Hate was dedicated to helping right-wing extremists move away from racist ideas and violent action. In June 2017, the funding for that program as rescinded by the Trump administration. There is no way of knowing whether it would have had any effect on the gunman who posted anti-Semitic comments on a right-wing social media platform shortly before murdering eleven worshippers at a Pittsburgh synagogue in October 2018. The FBI reported that right-wing extremists killed more Americans between 2010 and 2016 than any other domestic terrorists. I would argue that a smarter policy would be to take the learnings from the Obama years, such as those I describe above, and apply them to today's rapidly evolving threat environment. I will discuss specific proposals for adapting these programs to mass casualty events of all kinds, as well as the types of cyberinfiltrations we saw during the 2016 presidential election, in the final chapter.

PART III

WHERE WE NEED TO IMPROVE

CHAPTER 9

Connecting the Dots

On a beautiful spring day in March 2012, I found myself in a windowless room in the basement of the US Capitol. The thick metal door that could be opened only with a keypad sealed the room, known as a SCIF—a "sensitive compartmented information facility"—from electronic surveillance. I was sitting at a long table in the front of the room with the top cybersecurity officials of the Obama administration: John Brennan, the White House counterterrorism advisor; Robert Mueller, then director of the FBI; Attorney General Eric Holder; Secretary of Defense Leon Panetta; and General Keith Alexander, director of the National Security Agency and commander of the US Cyber Command. Arrayed in a semicircle around us were several dozen senators from both parties who had accepted a White House invitation for a briefing intended to illustrate the relative ease of crippling the United States without firing a shot.

The lights dimmed, and General Alexander began his presentation with an aerial shot of Manhattan, lights blazing against the night sky. In the next slide, a power company worker opens an email from a known address. With one keystroke, the kind made every day by millions of people around the world, the damage is done. A relatively unsophisticated "spear-phishing" attack is underway, and a malicious bug begins coursing through the power grid. Block by block,

Manhattan goes dark until it looks from the sky like North Korea does today. Meanwhile, utility workers scramble to find the cause of the blackout, unaware that one of their own has unwittingly started it.

The social and economic consequences of such an event are huge. A giant one-day blackout in New York City in 1977 led to looting, arson, and riots. In 2003, a two-day blackout that cascaded from failed power lines in Akron, Ohio, through the Midwest, the Northeast, and into Canada affected fifty-five million people and caused an estimated $10 billion in economic damage. It also knocked out digital communications networks, leading amateur ham radio operators to jump in and help first responders get information. Unlike these events, the power cutoff in General Alexander's scenario lasts for several days, with disruptions that cascade through critical infrastructure including the financial sector, telecommunications, air traffic control, the subway system, hospitals, homes, schools, businesses, ATMs, traffic lights, gas pumps, elevators, and every other aspect of modern life. The nation's largest city stops functioning. No one can get home, and no one knows what's coming next. What if cell phones and 911 fail too? Panic and chaos take over—it's the cyber equivalent of a 9/11.

These are the effects of an attack on one city, General Alexander cautioned. Terrorists don't have to commit mass murder to rack up a win. With the same ease and speed of the Manhattan scenario, skilled cyberattackers could simultaneously strike multiple American cities, plunging large sections of the United States into confusion and paralysis, bringing the economy and life as we know it to a standstill. The presentation wasn't necessarily designed to scare (though it certainly had that effect) but to educate the lawmakers in attention-grabbing detail about the real-world implications of a cyberattack on a US power grid—and to prod them into action.

At the time, the White House was trying to give a boost to stalled legislation intended to harden US critical infrastructure, such as power grids, telecommunications, and financial networks against cyberattack. General Alexander, a four-star army general whose intellectual and soft-spoken demeanor concealed astute political skills, made his case with characteristic military precision. After the lights came back on, there was a question-and-answer session. The senators wanted to know who had the capabilities to conduct such an attack, whether we knew of any previous attempts like the scenario they had just seen, and how we were prepared to respond should something like this happen. What they did not ask about was our opinion on the most effective thing that they could do. That would have been to pass a bill that set up a strong regulatory regime to ensure that our nation's critical infrastructure was as secure as possible. We offered that recommendation, but many of the lawmakers were not receptive at the time.

Private-sector companies now own and operate the vast majority of American critical infrastructure, including transportation; financial and communications networks; energy systems, such as refineries, dams, and power and water plants; nuclear, chemical, and manufacturing facilities; and hospitals. Companies include such household names as ConEdison, AT&T, Verizon, Citibank, JPMorgan Chase, Bank of America, Morgan Stanley, Dow Chemical, Boeing, Cisco, Oracle, Aetna, Anthem, and even professional sports leagues like the NFL, NBA, and MLB, which operate large public venues.

The Cybersecurity Act of 2012 was eventually defeated in the Senate. The Obama administration sought compromises, but many lawmakers and business interests, such as the US Chamber of Commerce, warned against excess regulation and government intrusion into the ways the private sector protects its own networks. Companies were not comfortable with the potential costs, and they were wary about sharing information with the government and competitors. Congress did eventually pass the Cybersecurity Act of 2015, which established cybersecurity information sharing among private-sector and federal government entities. It also reduces liability for companies that share cybersecurity information according to certain standards and take defensive measures to protect their networks, in the event they are sued for a data breach. The act also includes measures to boost the cybersecurity of critical information systems and networks.

One noteworthy thing, given our current security issues: neither the failed bill nor the one that passed designated voting systems, which are operated at the state level, as critical infrastructure. "Critical" was defined to mean "the interruption of life-sustaining services" or a mass casualty event, mass evacuations, catastrophic damage to the United States economy, or "severe degradation of national security capabilities."

Vladimir Putin seems to have parsed this exclusion shrewdly. In 2018, the Trump administration revealed that hackers connected to the Russian government infiltrated at least twenty state voting systems prior to the 2016 presidential election, and potentially twice that number, although it is still unclear to what effect. DHS detected the intrusions and, without naming the perpetrator, warned all fifty secretaries of state prior to the election about the potential for disruption.

There is no indication that the intruders did anything beyond accessing the systems—the equivalent of picking the lock, as opposed to coming through the door and turning the place upside down—but DHS officials were so concerned about the potential for vote tampering by foreign actors that the department set up a war room on election night, staffed by dozens of DHS cybersecurity experts and the FBI, to monitor for such events. As this book goes to print, no evidence yet indicates vote counts or certified election results were affected. That could of course change, and our intelligence agencies are unanimous in concluding that Russia poses an ongoing threat to local voting systems throughout the United States.

By today's standards, the hypothetical New York City blackout and our warnings in 2012 on behalf of the Obama administration of the dangers lurking seem quaint in some respects and frightfully prescient in others. In March 2018, the Trump administration imposed economic sanctions on Russia after revealing some of the evidence that Russian government cyberactors targeted multiple critical US infrastructure sectors, including energy, nuclear, water, aviation, and critical manufacturing. According to Symantec, a data security firm, the Russian efforts revealed in 2018 go back as far as 2011 and were launched by a hacking group it dubbed "Dragonfly" that targeted Western energy companies in the United States, Turkey, and Switzerland. This is another case of the hackers picking the locks of the companies' data networks, without actually launching an attack. That capability was exactly what we were trying to warn the lawmakers about in our not-so-hypothetical demonstration of an attack on the power grid.

As we saw during the Obama years, legislating in the cybersecurity arena is hard. Technology evolves so rapidly and the alliances and capabilities of good guys and bad guys change so often that policy makers struggle to get ahead of the curve. President Obama issued a series of executive orders, culminating in early 2016 with the Cybersecurity National Action Plan, which assigned DHS, the Department of Commerce, and the Department of Energy to set up a joint system for companies and organizations to test the security of their networks in a contained environment, for instance, by subjecting a replica power grid and attached communications networks to cyberattack. The plan also created a collaboration between DHS and Underwriters Laboratory (UL), the global safety science company, to test and certify networked smart devices, such as home appliances and medical devices, to ensure they meet certain digital safety standards.

This was a case where we made efforts to be forward-looking—for instance, by making sure pacemakers can't be hacked (a scenario straight out of the TV series *Homeland*)—but bad actors were largely operating freely in other online arenas. We know now that by early 2016, Cambridge Analytica, the defunct British political-consulting and data-mining firm at the heart of the Facebook election scandal, was gathering vast amounts of user information that would be used to target online political ads aimed at benefiting the Trump campaign. It is a scenario that might have seemed far-fetched to us even a few years ago. Now it's our reality.

The Russians, the Chinese, and other adversaries understand the importance of cyberspace to our democracy, our economic prosperity, and our way of life. China has for years had government doctrine to create pressure on US companies and government agencies to change policies they do not like. In 2018, China's Cyberspace Administration ordered Marriott to take down its website in China after the hotel chain included Taiwan and Tibet, which China regards as breakaway provinces, in a pull-down menu of countries. Marriott apologized, and its website was restored after a week. Similar scoldings have been issued to US airlines for listing Taiwan on their websites.

Russia favors attacks on critical infrastructure, such as power, communications, and voting systems, of democratic rivals. Hackers connected to the Russian government executed attacks against the power grid in Ukraine in 2015 and 2016, causing widespread electrical outages and related disruptions of communications networks, in a modern show of force. Without reliable communications, the damage and response time are magnified exponentially, as we also saw in Puerto Rico following Hurricane Maria in 2017.

Russia, China, and North Korea, among other adversaries, are experts in a type of network attack known as an advanced persistent threat. The intruders gain a foothold in a victim's system, and they watch, learn, and wait for a moment to strike. They test their acquired knowledge on other countries, as Russia did with Ukraine or China has done in Taiwan. Sometimes they strike directly, as North Korea did in an infamous attack exposing the emails of Sony Picture executives when the studio produced a movie ridiculing a fictional North Korean leader in 2014. As the geopolitical winds change, so do the roster of perpetrators and targets. In 2018, *Bloomberg Businessweek* reported that China conducted a sophisticated hardware hack by installing spyware in computer components that were manufactured in China and later exported to the United States, where they were installed into sensitive servers sold by US government subcontractors as well as private companies, including Apple and Amazon. Apple and Amazon denied their hardware was hacked, but it is not hard to see the vulnerabilities of a global supply chain that originates within the borders of a nation that is a key economic and political rival.

With the proliferation of threats and capabilities in cyberspace, there is no clear doctrine as we had during the Cold War, for instance, when the United States engaged consistently in a policy of containing Soviet influence, regardless of which political party was in power. As a government, we cannot yet agree on a definition or on principles governing cyberspace. In the minds of defense and national-security players, it is a military dimension, along with land, sea, air, and space. From the perspective of DHS, it is a civilian space for commerce, communication, and knowledge. Everyone is correct—cyberspace has both civilian and military dimensions. We are most vulnerable in combatting adversaries like Russia who weaponize the civilian aspects of critical infrastructure, whether that means election systems or power grids.

Our fractured cybersecurity command structure means that it's not only DHS that has responsibility; it's also the jurisdiction of the FBI, the Department of Defense, and even the Department of Commerce, which helps to promote the development of cybersecurity technologies and practices in the private sector. While the Department of Defense has the lead for all military networks, through the US Cyber Command, there is not a single department on the front line in the civilian sector of government. DHS is the lead agency for critical infrastructure involving transportation, communications, and manufacturing. Treasury is the lead for the financial sector, the Department of Energy for power plants, the Department of Agriculture for food, and so on.

At the end of the day, though, the private sector is in the lead in the civilian sector, and the government agencies provide support as needed. A company whose system is hacked may need help from the FBI in figuring out who did it and how to prosecute, but they turn to DHS if they want help in securing their network using best industry practices or in alerting others to ongoing danger. The key here is that all of this government activity is voluntary. A company or organization has to ask the government to come help. Some, wary of compromising trade secrets through information sharing or suffering reputational damage, choose not to.

We see similar reluctance in the public sector as well. Some local government officials viewed DHS involvement in the security of their systems during the 2016 presidential election as a federal takeover. The secretary of state of Georgia, a Republican, likened the DHS election warning to an expansion of federal power akin to Obamacare. The secretary of state of Vermont, a Democrat, said DHS involvement in voting was a "nose in the tent thing" by Washington, implying that the federal government was improperly intruding on state business. We cannot seem to get out of our own way. In the final weeks of his administration, President Obama instructed my successor, Jeh Johnson, to designate election systems as critical infrastructure. DHS now has oversight through its organization monitoring the cybersecurity of government facilities. In effect though, the best DHS could do in this case was to close the barn door after the horses had run.

The challenge with election security is that elections are local events, administered by counties, often relying on antiquated infrastructure. The complexity is profound. Going into the 2020 presidential election, we have at least forty states that need to update and secure their systems. The challenge is to develop an election system that has security baked in from the beginning, before any foreign actor can penetrate the networks and wait to make trouble. We've heard so much from the Trump administration about the country being "infested" or "invaded" by immigrants who enter our country unlawfully, to seek asylum, the chance to work, or to be reunited with loved ones. What our true adversaries are doing silently and out of sight on our data networks is far more dangerous.

Caitlin Durkovich was my assistant secretary for infrastructure protection at DHS. Upbeat and energetic, she also approached her work with a seriousness consistent with the gravity of her responsibilities. So when Caitlin reported to me on the confusion that existed during government briefings to the private companies who control nearly all of American critical infrastructure, I knew we had a problem. Caitlin would describe what she saw at government briefings, imagining the perspective of a private company. "You'd have somebody from the FBI; you'd have somebody from DHS; maybe you'd have someone from the governor's office; you'd talk about cybersecurity," Caitlin said. "I'd finish my brief and I say, 'Call us. We've got tools.' Then the FBI guy would stand up and say, 'Duh-duh-duh-duh-duh, and by the way, call us.' Then the governor's office would say, 'By the way, call us.' If you're a member of the private sector, you're like, 'What the hell is going on here?'"

I saw two major challenges. First, we had jurisdictional issues within the federal government. As the lead law-enforcement agency, the FBI had more experience than DHS and a lot more swagger too. But their approach is organized around criminal investigations and prosecutions. Cybersecurity involves a spectrum of measures taken to prepare a company or organization to prevent, protect, mitigate, respond to, and recover from cyberattack. The FBI has a clear role in the prevention phase by catching cyberattackers, but DHS is better suited for the other steps on the spectrum, making it harder to hack systems in the first place and helping organizations better understand the threats emanating from cyberspace and providing timely, actionable information to protect their networks.

Second, regardless of which government agency was in charge, the private sector is more nimble in developing and adapting new technologies to protect their networks. As we learned from the failed cybersecurity legislation in 2012 and subsequent efforts, US companies do not want a lead regulatory agency that sets industry standards for cybersecurity, the way, for example, the Securities and Exchange Commission regulates the financial industry in the United States. This leaves us with our current system, if that's what we can call it, of voluntary partnership between industry and government.

In recent years, companies have developed more of a healthy appreciation of the threats caused by inadequate cybersecurity in terms of financial, operational, and reputational risk. But because it is so hard to touch and feel these problems and fixing them is so complex and expensive, cybersecurity is still seen as a cost center rather than a worthwhile investment. Most CEOs do not have an IT background, so when they consider whether to buy a new turbine or invest in security, the turbine takes priority. Security involves many layers and tools. It's hard for companies to navigate at the end of the day. As in data privacy, the best solution is prevention: security by design rather than costly and ineffective security retrofitting of data networks.

For all of these reasons, I am going to mark a giant red "needs improvement" in the homeland security report card. Incursions into critical infrastructure, voting technology, and social media show that our vulnerabilities are deep and deepening, as the technological capabilities of our adversaries and their political willingness to use cyberweapons have become more pronounced by the day. And a dangerous pattern has emerged. As we did in the run-up to 9/11, we now live in an era of constant probing. Our adversaries want to find out how far they can get before being detected or stopped. In 1993, we saw the first attack on the World Trade Center, a bomb that killed six and injured a thousand people, by terrorists who were part of the same network later responsible for the 9/11 attacks. In 1998, al-Qaeda operatives bombed the US embassies in Kenya and Tanzania, killing two hundred, and they attacked the USS *Cole* in Yemen, killing thirty-nine. Late in August 2001, US intelligence intercepted chatter by associates of Osama bin Laden that "something big" was being planned. We found out what that big thing was less than three weeks later.

The antecedent in this case is the attack on the 2016 election. Russian activities during our 2016 election clearly constituted interference and demonstrate the need for a stronger response by the United States to what can only be construed as a state-sponsored attack on our country, where we have no evidence that they have stopped. We have to ask ourselves: what are they planning next? "The most important failure was one of imagination," the 9/11 Commission concluded in its report after the catastrophe. "We do not believe leaders understood the gravity of the threat." The cascade of cyberattacks leaves little to the imagination anymore, and officials in the government are showing the same lack of attention to these issues as they did in the weeks and months before 9/11.

Once again, as the government failed to do before 9/11, no one is connecting the dots. As a country we are not prepared for the cyber equivalent of 9/11—and it's time to close the gap. Unlike a conventional military strike, a cyberattack requires little in the way of government or financial resources. For our power grid scenario in 2012, we used tools that are freely available on the internet to show lawmakers that it costs little to nothing to launch a successful attack. Bad actors need no financiers, no banking trails, nothing other than an internet connection, malicious code, and an understanding of their victims' vulnerabilities to wreak havoc. Unlike conventional terrorist attacks, a cyberattacker does not need a bomb maker to rig up the hardware and get it into the hands of terrorists. The open-source tools of destruction are highly democratized and available to all. As Obama concluded in 2016, "Criminals, terrorists and countries who wish to do us harm have all realized that attacking us online is often easier than attacking us in person."

In addition to the disruption of the 2016 presidential election by Russian-controlled social media bots and the hacking of state voting systems, there is a growing list of spectacular data breaches involving the private sector. Companies such as Target, Sony, Equifax, Yahoo!, Fannie Mae, United Healthcare, Anthem, and others have fallen victim. The Office of Personnel Management lost background information, including fingerprints and social security numbers, of an estimated 22 million current and prospective employees in 2015. While the most notorious attacks threaten our democracy itself, others threaten to destabilize our society and our economy. Some are just plain embarrassing, revealing the foibles of corporate executives and US diplomats and trade secrets and compromising hundreds of millions of American consumers at a time. One of the largest private-sector breaches involved Adult FriendFinder, an online dating and "hookup" site for single and married people, that affected 412 million users. By comparison, the data theft from Equifax, the consumer credit-rating agency, involved 143 million consumers. I will leave it to the social scientists rather than us national-security types to figure out what that tells us about our society.

The US government struggles along with the private sector. The National Security Agency saw an embarrassing lapse involving the theft of its own cyberweapons, which were then used in ransomware attacks in 2017 that targeted hospitals and private companies worldwide. One such attack caused the brief shutdown of the British National Health Service. While it may not always seem like it, the National Security Agency is in fact a global leader in cyberintelligence. The problem is that its weapons and intelligence are part of US national-security networks, where different laws and limitations apply, and they do not connect to civilian government networks. This is yet another reason for departments and parts of government to work in tandem—something we are failing at. Unlike military intelligence, there are no clear rules for gathering, analyzing, and sharing cyberintelligence among government decision makers. Agencies like the CIA, the FBI, and the National Security Agency are still operating in silos.

It's not hard to imagine the public safety implications. In April 2017, someone managed to flip on all 156 tornado sirens in Dallas, causing fear and confusion and flooding the 911 system with thousands of calls. The perpetrator was later revealed to be a "white hat" hacker in San Francisco, who used a laptop and a $35 radio to make a point: anyone armed with the same know-how could make sirens play whatever audio they programmed, including false warnings of tsunamis or incoming missiles. These are only the attacks we have heard about. According to a report released in 2017 by the firm Security Scorecard, US federal, state, and local government agencies rank in last place in cybersecurity when compared against major private industries, including transportation, retail, and health care. Of the six hundred government agencies tracked, NASA performed the worst. Other low-performing government organizations included the US Department of State and the information systems used by the states of Connecticut, Pennsylvania, Washington, and even the county of Maricopa in my home state of Arizona.

While I am not a fan of exposing vulnerabilities in ways that risk public panic, for instance, flipping on tornado sirens, healthy paranoia is needed in both government and industry. We should hire our own white hat hackers. False assumptions and biases make every organization vulnerable. Cyberattacks are today a matter of when, not if, and you want to make sure you have done all you can to protect your most critical assets.

Our persistent vulnerability to a major cyberattack is frightening on many levels. It can be intended as an act of war—silent, unexpected, and devastating. It can be ransomware designed for commercial gain or even mischief. There may be multiple motives, and they are sometimes hard to discern. And it's often very difficult to identify the perpetrators. It's hard for the victim to know in the moment if they are dealing with an individual, a group of individuals, individuals authorized by the state, or with a nation-state directly, which often gets in the way of an immediate response.

National borders are insignificant, since it takes only moments in some cases for malware to make its way around the world. So without something akin to arms-control conventions like we had during the Cold War, there is no way to prevent escalation in cyber-warfare. Russia hacks our presidential election; we turn around and hack their oil industry. They respond by hacking our power grid; we bring their foreign currency exchanges to a halt. The proverbial red phone that used to connect the superpowers during the Cold War is useless in this situation.

Recognizing the risks of uncontrolled escalation, in 2018 a group of American companies led by Microsoft president Brad Smith and backed by Cisco, HP, and Facebook, as well as the European companies Nokia, ABB, and ARM, took a step toward a "Digital Geneva Convention." The companies pledged they would not help governments conduct cyberattacks against "innocent citizens and enterprises" and that they would assist governments and others under cyberattack. The cybersecurity tech accord did not define who qualifies as "innocent," and it has not gotten unanimous support in the industry. Industry giants, including Apple, Amazon, and Google, have not signed the pledge as of this writing.

It's an unbelievably complicated set of problems. But we are a nation of problem solvers, and we don't have a choice. Think what harm might have been prevented if the 9/11 Commission had existed and asked all of its tough questions *before* 9/11. We know enough now to identify the issues that a true cybersecurity homeland defense must address. What we need to begin with is a Committee on Cybersecurity of the Homeland (a pre-9/11 Commission, if you will), convened by the president and appointing the best and brightest from the government and private sectors. The commission should be charged with answering ten fundamental questions:

1. What are the precise roles and responsibilities of the agencies of the federal government where cybersecurity is concerned, including the Departments of Defense, State, Commerce, Justice,

and Homeland Security; the FBI, the CIA, and the National Security Agency?

2. How is cyberintelligence best collected and disseminated to relevant decision makers?

3. What are the vulnerabilities of the nation's critical infrastructure, and how can they best be addressed?

4. How can federally gathered cyberintelligence most effectively be shared with the private sector and with state and local governments? How are cyberwarnings best delivered, by whom, and in what format?

5. In the event cyberintelligence is collected by the private sector or by state and local governments, how should it most effectively be shared with the federal government? Which federal agencies should receive it?

6. What private-sector standards should be established for cybersecurity purposes? Should they be mandatory or voluntary? Who should set the standards, and how should they be kept up to date?

7. In the event of a successful cyberattack on critical infrastructure, who is responsible for coordinating the response? The recovery?

8. What are the rules of engagement where an attack is attributed to a state or to a state-sponsored actor? What constitutes a declaration of war in the cyber context?

9. What are the ranges of countermeasures, including economic sanctions and counterattacks, that should be deployed in the event of a successful cyberattack by a state or a state-sponsored actor?

10. What international efforts or organizations should be involved for purposes of establishing a global charter for the protection of cyberspace? What are the rules governing relations between nations where cyberspace is concerned? Is such an international effort worth pursuing?

There are no easy answers; I know. One challenge, we learned quite painfully during Facebook CEO Mark Zuckerberg's testimony before a panel of much older senators is that those familiar with the technology are often limited in their understanding of the policy and legal framework in which our government operates. And the policy makers, not to mention our legal decision makers, are often limited in their understanding of how digital technology works. Technology advances far more quickly than does our policy and legal machinery.

In addition to a Cybersecurity Commission, a cyber-FEMA within DHS should be established. Where natural disasters are concerned, FEMA gives out grants to localities for training and exercises. A cyber-FEMA could perform a similar function, ensuring that communities have the basic necessities to function until critical infrastructure operators can get their systems back up and functioning. Since a cyberattack may not result in physical damage that the public can see and understand, the role of any government should be to help people understand what is going on and to manage expectations while industry applies its expertise to solve the problem. For instance, the US Geological Survey publishes an annual report showing residents of earthquake zones in California how long they may have to wait for the restoration of water and power services, depending on the location of their property and the projected severity of an earthquake. This knowledge, unsettling as it is, helps residents who bother to read the study to be prepared by stockpiling enough water, batteries, and other interim power sources. While such a projection is more difficult for a cyberattack, as there are so many unknowns, accurate information is always useful in a crisis.

Another idea worth thinking about is how to incentivize the private sector to invest more in their own security infrastructure. Because security expenditures do not generate an identifiable return on investment, there is a tendency to underinvest. This tendency is what makes a voluntary regime of security standards so problematic, although it is the system we currently have. Congress could consider extending a federal tax credit for investments in cybersecurity as a means of incentivizing such investment. Alternatively, Congress could consider some form of federal insurance that could be purchased by companies that invest in their own cybersecurity. Even though this sets a relatively low bar, it would be a start. And we can move, as has the European Union, toward a regulatory regime for cybersecurity. Efforts to adopt such policies have failed in the United States so far and have gained little traction, even following the Cambridge Analytica personal data collection scandal. When Zuckerberg testified before Congress about it, there was the bizarre spectacle of senators asking him how they should best regulate his company. "My position is that there should be no regulation," he responded. (I'm glad we got that settled.)

The best thing we can do is invest in security by design at the front end and reward companies that do so with tax and other benefits. One option is to extend the liability protections of the DHS SAFETY Act, which applies to the builders of physical structures who meet certain standards designed to reduce the threat of terrorism and includes digital networks as well. In this way, companies who invest in secure and resilient cybersystems will receive a designation that gives them greater liability protection in case there is a cyberattack against them and a customer or user of their system sues. This will incentivize security by design. This approach will be helped through "biodigital convergence," involving the use of biometric data, such as fingerprints and iris scans, to authenticate authorized users.

It is impossible to overstate the urgency of improving our country's cybersecurity. After climate change, there is no greater threat to the homeland. This is not to say that terrorism has been eradicated or that the threat from lone wolves and mass shooters is not significant, but the threats of attack on our critical infrastructure are so far-reaching and our defenses so inadequate that we cannot continue with business as usual. The frequency, intensity, and sophistication of attempted attacks by our adversaries only increase. When I began as DHS secretary in 2009, I spent maybe 10 percent of my time on cyberrelated matters. By the time I left in 2013, probably 40 percent of my time was devoted to cybersecurity issues. I know that's only increased for my successors. This threat requires that we be more agile, more organized, and more forward-thinking. Our survival is at stake.

CHAPTER 10

Black Swans and Oily Ducks

In March 2009, a few weeks after I was sworn in at DHS, nearly all of North Dakota experienced record flooding. Along the Missouri River, water levels were so high that local officials needed explosives to blow up ice floes near Bismarck to expedite the flow of floodwater downstream. The next month, the Centers for Disease Control reported the first US case of a new form of swine flu, known as H1N1, which was first detected in Veracruz, Mexico. The first US patient was a ten-year-old child in California, followed two days later by an eight-year-old, also in California, who had no known contact with the first child patient—or with pigs. Within days, H1N1 cases affecting people appeared in Kansas, Ohio, and New York. Unlike other flu strains, H1N1 struck young people more severely than those over sixty years old. We were looking at a potential pandemic, perhaps the most severe since the worldwide influenza outbreak of 1918.

Then, on April 20, 2010, the oil rig Deepwater Horizon exploded in the Gulf of Mexico, killing eleven crewmen and injuring another seventeen. Two days later, the rig sank, and oil began leaking from the seabed, one mile beneath the surface of the gulf. By the time the well was capped almost five months later, some 4.9 million gallons of crude oil had poured into the Gulf of Mexico, imperiling marine life and beaches from Louisiana to Florida and disrupting the local tourism and fishing economies. It became the worst accidental oil spill in world history. (The *Exxon Valdez*, by comparison, dumped 750,000 gallons into the Prince William Sound off Alaska in 1989.)

I had more than a few "What have I gotten myself into?" moments during that first year or so, which turned out to be an omen for my time at the Department of Homeland Security. Events like the ones mentioned above are "black swans," defined by the philosopher and statistician Nassim Taleb as having three attributes. "First, it is an outlier, as it lies outside the realm of regular expectations, because nothing in the past can convincingly point to its possibility. Second, it carries an extreme impact. . . . Third, in spite of its outlier status, human nature makes us concoct explanations for its occurrence after the fact, making it explainable and predictable."

For instance, we know that the rivers in North Dakota are prone to flooding, but we did not predict that flooding would be compounded by late-season ice storms on top of frozen and saturated ground and that floods would take place not only in one watershed but in dozens simultaneously throughout the northern plains. Flu season rolls around every year, but rarely do we see a virus jump from livestock to humans, with no known vaccine. Oil spills are not that rare, but we have never seen one originating in such deep water that defied capping for so long. Only the Gulf War oil spill of 1991 saw a greater release, causing as much as eleven million gallons of crude to pour into the Persian Gulf, but that was caused by Iraqi troops opening a pipeline as they retreated from Kuwait, apparently to foil a landing by US Marines. This environmental catastrophe was an act of war, not an industrial accident like the Deepwater Horizon. We understand now that both episodes are possible, but neither incident was predicted.

Throughout my tenure at DHS, we managed a veritable flock of black swans, most caused by natural disasters. But these were not anomalies. Natural disasters are taking an ever-greater toll in lives and money each year around the world. Just days before Hurricane Sandy decimated the Eastern Seaboard in 2012, the International Monetary Fund reported that seven hundred natural disasters affecting more than 450 million people were registered between 2000 and 2010 and that damages per event had risen from an average of $20 billion per year in the 1990s to about $100 billion per year. That is a fivefold increase in only a decade. This upward trend is expected to continue as a result of the rising numbers of people living in areas exposed to natural disasters and the increasing frequency and severity of extreme weather events due to climate change. According to the United Nations, the number of events requiring a disaster declaration has more than quadrupled to about four hundred a year worldwide, with more than one taking place now each day.

The trends in the United States follow a similar pattern. The National Oceanic and Atmospheric Administration (NOAA) tracks climate-related losses for the Department of Commerce. In 2017, NOAA reported that since 1980, the United States has sustained 219 weather and climate disasters in which overall damages reached or exceeded $1 billion. In 1980, there were 3 such events. By contrast, in 2017, there were 16 events in this category. The cumulative damage of these 16 disasters, which included Hurricane Harvey in Texas, Hurricane Irma in Florida, and Hurricane Maria in Puerto Rico and the Caribbean, as well as record wildfires in the West, made 2017 the costliest year on record for natural disasters in the United States. In 2018, we again saw epic devastation from Hurricane Florence in the Carolinas and Hurricane Michael, a rare category 4 storm that hit the Florida panhandle.

Despite these losses, we have made tremendous progress in mitigating natural disasters since Hurricane Katrina in 2005, when the failure of government of all levels led to the deaths of more than eighteen hundred residents along the Gulf Coast, destroyed New Orleans, and laid bare the terrible shortcomings of the Federal

Emergency Management Agency (FEMA). We have done much to fix FEMA and improve coordination among the federal, state, and local governments who are first responders in a disaster. But as is often the case with homeland security, the problem set has shifted. Just as it is no longer sufficient to prepare and defend against a single, massive, centrally coordinated terrorist attack, such as we saw on 9/11, neither can we gird ourselves for a certain number of "hundred-year" or "five-hundred-year" or even "thousand-year" events, such as Hurricane Harvey, which dumped more than fifty inches of rain on Houston in September 2017, exceeding in only four days the city's annual rainfall. This thousand-year event was followed within weeks by Hurricane Irma in Florida and Hurricane Maria, which devastated the US island of Puerto Rico and many Caribbean nations. In California, the deadliest wildfires in state history took place one year apart, in 2017 and 2018. Designations once intended to convey rarity are losing their meaning.

As with terrorism in the post-9/11 era, we live in a different threat environment, one shaped by climate change. For every politician who throws a snowball on the floor of the US Senate, as Oklahoma senator James Inhofe did in 2015, to prove that "eggheads at science laboratories" were wrong to claim the earth was warming, I don't need to rely on an army of "eggheads" to prove the opposite. The scientific data is backed by the daily experiences of thousands upon thousands of American farmers, ranchers, fishermen, loggers, sailors, marines and Coast Guard members, and any number of commonsense people who work the land and the oceans. Vermont was lashed by Tropical Storm Irene in 2016, for heaven's sake. New England has become hurricane country. Droughts and wildfires in the West grow more intense each decade. Climate change is here, and it is not going anywhere, and its truly horrifying to know that the number of policy makers in this country who deny climate change is not insignificant.

While DHS has made significant progress in the post-9/11 era to deter terrorists and secure our borders, we are spinning our wheels on perhaps the biggest threat to the homeland of all. Unlike every other threat we face, climate change is irreversible. Once the damage is done, no amount of expertise, money, or military might can fix it. This deepening vulnerability results from static partisan battles (much like those we have over immigration), as well as the human tendency to fail to act when one threat seems less immediate or potent than another. If a guy tries to blow up his underwear on a plane, we leap into action. Yet if the waters begin to rise around our coastal cities or wildfires creep from our western forests into the suburbs, we respond to these incidents one by one rather than taking a systems approach.

Instead of adopting policies on energy, building, land management, urban planning, flood control, and insurance that would mitigate the threat from climate change over the long term, we pour hundreds of billions of dollars into reacting to and recovering from climate-driven disasters. Then we task FEMA with issuing insurance payments to rebuild homes and businesses in flood plains or in increasingly vulnerable coastal areas or on the ever larger and more dangerous urban-wildland interfaces that burn as our cities continue to sprawl in arid regions of the country. If President Trump wants to build a "big, beautiful wall" to protect the United States, he should at least make it a seawall.

FEMA was radically overhauled after the catastrophic failures of Hurricane Katrina in 2005, and this transformation is one of the greatest accomplishments of the Department of Homeland Security. When I made my first visit to New Orleans as DHS secretary in 2009 to check on the recovery effort that was then in its fourth year, FEMA employees were in a post-Katrina funk. I remember many of them were actually embarrassed to wear their government-issued polo shirts with the agency logo. I launched a nationwide search for a new FEMA administrator, and the same name kept popping up: Craig Fugate, head of the Florida Emergency Management Division, under command of then Florida governor Jeb Bush. Craig was not too polished; he didn't have the resume of the typical political appointees who land high positions in the US government. Craig was gruff, a native Floridian from Jacksonville, who trained as a volunteer fire-fighter and a paramedic, before working his way into emergency management. He went around in a University of Florida Gators sweatshirt and baseball hat and was the only guy I knew who some-how got away with not wearing a tie to meetings at the White House. But Craig knew his stuff. President Obama came to really respect him, as did we all, and with a wink dubbed him the "the idiot savant of disasters."

One of the first things Fugate did was to whip FEMA headquarters into shape. He found dispirited employees paralyzed by the fear of "another Katrina." Decisions were made slowly, if at all, and many FEMA workers seemed more worried about how their email or com-ments in a meeting might come across in a future, imagined congres-sional hearing than accomplishing their mission. Fugate recognized the bias in government was to not take action, not make a mistake, and not be accused of fraud, waste, and abuse. The default position was to avoid doing anything that might make the agency look inept. They'd had enough of that already. But in a fast-moving crisis, deci-sions need to be made quickly in the field, plans get redrawn in an instant, and the lines of command and control have to be clear.

There is simply no time to obsess over past mistakes. I learned this myself from President Obama's response during the underwear bomber episode. He was focused on moving forward and fixing the problem, not on whose fault it was. One of the key mistakes during the response to Hurricane Katrina was that the Bush administration waited too long for the governor of Louisiana and the mayor of New Orleans to formally request federal aid rather than sending life-saving assets ahead of the storm. It is easier to pre-position water, rations, generators, and other relief supplies than to haul them later into a disaster zone aboard high-water trucks and boats or airlift them. Of course, FEMA, state offices of emergency response, the Red Cross, and other relief agencies store such supplies in many places around the country, but it is a matter of scale. A category 5 storm requires category 5 preparation.

Craig was fond of a saying by Dwight D. Eisenhower, when he was Allied commander in Europe and the US Army's only five-star general: "Plans are worthless, but planning is everything." Fugate despised the federal government's disaster-planning exercises, in which top officials work through thick binders of emergency scenarios and recite scripted responses as "bad Shakespearean plays." As a former governor, I couldn't agree more. Instead of role-playing that was scheduled during business hours, Craig instituted "Thunderbolt" exercises, no-notice drills that might take place on evenings or weekends or during the morning commute or even, once, when employees were milling on the sidewalk outside headquarters during a fire alarm. Those who didn't have their laptops or phones on them soon learned to be prepared. One day, when the power went out at FEMA headquarters, Craig insisted on the spot that his operations team head to a continuity facility located far from downtown DC and continue working. When the team fretted that the power outage might end while they were still stuck in traffic to the other site, he responded, "Or it might not." It was that mind-set to be prepared for anything that Craig wanted to instill. And he succeeded.

Craig and I wanted to send a message. As with many of the agencies under DHS, FEMA was getting a cultural overhaul to create a bias for action. FEMA employees were empowered to reach out to state and local authorities to offer aid rather than waiting for formal requests to filter up from local governments. Much of FEMA's work consists of breaking out its checkbook and reimbursing state and local governments for their recovery to disasters of a certain magnitude. We focused instead on scenarios when the federal government's response was needed before or during the disaster itself. Craig spoke in terms that people understood. He devised the "Waffle House Index" in southern states to determine how bad a storm was. If the local breakfast spot was open, even if it was serving a limited menu, emergency workers should keep going until they reached a community or neighborhood where the Waffle House could not open due to the disaster and set up base there.

The clear thinking paid off. When the Deepwater Horizon exploded, the Obama administration declared the incident a spill of national significance, designating DHS as the agency in command and the Coast Guard as incident commander. With clear and immediate lines of command and control, we were able to move forty thousand federal workers to the Gulf Coast within two weeks, find housing for a small city's worth of personnel, bring necessary vessels through the Panama Canal, and organize a team at the principal level, including myself, the secretaries of the Departments of the Interior and Energy, the administrator of the EPA, the White House, and the Coast Guard incident commander.

We initially spoke twice a day by phone, regardless of where we happened to be in the world, in whichever time zone, to make sure we had the same set of facts and to coordinate the responses of our federal agencies with the state and local first responders. Sometimes we just took care of questions at the principal level.

Question from the EPA administrator: Should the EPA authorize the use of chemical dispersants on the oil slick headed for the Gulf Coast?

Answer: Yes.

That was a key learning from the *Exxon Valdez* spill in 1989, which saw days wasted while toxic crude spread across Prince William Sound. With a decision made in minutes, our operations teams then executed the decision within hours.

Speed is the name of the game. Speed builds momentum and response. It gives FEMA the ability to quickly get to where the needs are and support the survivors. But speed also instills a bit of confidence in your superiors, in this case in the White House, so the president and his staff could see what the federal government was doing and that we were doing it well, making political leaders less inclined to intervene as a result. Only once did President Obama intervene, and that was after a flyover of the spill zone a few days after the explosion, when he came back and said to the team managing the federal government response, "Guys, we need more people down there." We sent them immediately.

My team and I were frustrated at times, though, that the media coverage did not reflect the breadth of our response. We were bringing massive federal resources to bear on the largest accidental oil spill in world history but losing the battle of perception. The worldwide media interest was intense. The BBC covered the incident nonstop, driven in part by the gaffe-prone CEO of BP, the British multinational that owned the platform. (Tony Hayward's most famous line: "I'd like my life back.") The AP opened a Gulf Coast bureau to cover the spill. CNN carried a nonstop video feed of the underwater oil plume and a timer in the corner of the screen tracking how long it had been gushing.

We kept a TV on in one of our field offices, in part to track where CNN anchor Anderson Cooper was reporting. We knew that Cooper, who was always in a black muscle t-shirt, was looking for stories of government incompetence. Once, we were appalled to see him doing a report from a polluted beach; pointing to a forlorn, oil-covered duck; and stating, "FEMA is nowhere to be found." In fact, a cleanup crew was just out of the camera angle, waiting for him to finish his standup shot so they could go in and help. We became somewhat cynical after that. Those were long and hard days, and in our fatigue and frustration, we came up with our own conspiracy theory that the journalists were handing around the same bedraggled waterfowl. We imagined the photographer saying to Cooper, "Hey, are you done with the duck? We have to shoot a magazine cover for *Newsweek*."

To be sure, FEMA is not perfect; nor is there a Waffle House everywhere in the country. Yet there are events we already know have a high likelihood of occurring, like a truly deadly pandemic, for which we remain ill prepared. One of the little-known responsibilities of DHS is to coordinate the federal response to instances of pandemic. We were fortunate in 2009 as H1N1 did not turn out to have the high mortality rate we initially feared. Had it been as lethal as the Spanish flu of 1918, the country would have been in real trouble. It takes time to identify vaccines for new flu strains and even more time to manufacture and distribute them.

To my dismay, I discovered that the United States is no longer a major vaccine manufacturer. Much production shifted from Europe to India and China starting around 2009 so that even when manufacture of a critical vaccine began, we would be competing on the global market with buyers in other countries for supply. Our disaster relief plans depend on being able to muster resources from other communities to assist when one community is in need. In case of pandemic, however, the impacts are felt everywhere, so there are no additional resources to contribute. In 2009, while Health and Human Services Secretary Kathleen Sebelius worked on vaccine issues and Secretary of Education Arne Duncan worked on questions like whether we should close the nation's schools as a preventative measure (we didn't, in part, because states, not the federal government, operate schools), I worked on communications with the public, emphasizing our most effective and basic remedy—wash your hands and cough into your elbow.

In this arena, we must also enable our public health and homeland security system to deal with the threat of pandemic, whether caused by nature or a biological attack perpetrated by a bad actor. Although the likelihood of such an event is unlikely, or, more accurately, unknown, the magnitude of such an event would be immense. Our narrow miss with H1N1 swine flu in 2009 revealed a vulnerable infrastructure with inadequate capabilities to quarantine the sick, manufacture vaccines, set up a supply chain of critical equipment (like ventilators), decontaminate public spaces, train medical personnel, and communicate with the public without creating panic.

We updated a thin playbook, but DHS cannot fix the fragility of our health care infrastructure. Assets are unevenly distributed, and it is hard to stockpile the right quantities of the right vaccines in the right places.

The threats described above are real, and many, though not all, are the result of climate change. This is not quick-fix stuff, and remedies defy slogans that fit on the brim of a baseball hat. Addressing climate change means investing in new technologies, adjusting our energy diet and our lifestyle, and adopting mitigation strategies, like new zoning and building codes. Hardly vote getters. Climate change gets lots of attention, but it does not evoke the urgent emotional response of terrorism for most people—or, for others, immigration. We see less action as a result. But climate change threatens our way of life in ways more far-reaching and permanent than anything else. Any secretary of homeland security who is diverted from this existential threat to chase down imagined threats or less deadly ones is falling down on the job. Americans need to be aware of this and demand leadership that will bring the full powers of the federal government and the private sector to bear. This is an area where our 325 million American partners are needed as critically as anywhere else.

PART IV

HOMELAND SECURITY IN THE AGE OF TRUMP

CHAPTER 11

Are We Safer?

At 8:07 a.m. local time on January 13, 2018, every smartphone screen in Hawaii lit up with a single message all in caps: "BALLISTIC MISSILE THREAT INBOUND TO HAWAII. SEEK IMMEDIATE SHELTER. THIS IS NOT A DRILL." In the same instant, television stations in Hawaii started carrying a screen crawl reading, in part, "The US Pacific Command has detected a missile threat to Hawaii. A missile may impact on land or sea within minutes. THIS IS NOT A DRILL. If you are indoors, stay indoors. If you are outdoors, seek immediate shelter in a building. Remain indoors well away from windows. If you are driving, pull safely to the side of the road and seek shelter in a nearby building or lay on the floor." Audio of the warning was carried on radio as well. Screenshots of the alert ricocheted worldwide on Twitter.

As the world now knows, the false missile alarm was triggered by a confused worker at the Hawaii Emergency Management Agency headquarters in Diamond Head Crater, who mistook instructions he received during an unscheduled emergency drill for a real attack. The mishap occurred at the end of a week that had seen unusually aggressive rhetoric between North Korean leader Kim Jong Un and President Donald Trump. Hawaii lies forty-six hundred miles across the Pacific Ocean from North Korea, an estimated twelve- to fifteen-minute missile flight, so the errant warning provoked more excitement than it may have had it taken place in Kansas.

On Oahu, motorists drove erratically as they raced to park their cars inside a freeway tunnel. At one ecoranch in Kaneohe, tourists took shelter in a mountainside bunker. Spectators fled sporting events, and college students ran to campus tsunami shelters. The 911 system jammed in many areas, as did wireless data services, making it difficult for people to get accurate information from the internet. Panicked parents whose children were at different schools chose which child to pick up in the time available before the end they thought was coming. Some people opened manhole covers in search of a fallout shelter. Others called or texted loved ones to say good-bye.

Within minutes of the alert, commanders of the Hawaii National Guard and the US Pacific Command were in communication, as were members of the Hawaii congressional delegation, local police chiefs, and mayors throughout the state, confirming in numerous separate conversations that it was a false alarm. Various authorities began sending out social media messages to that effect, but it was not until 8:38 a.m. that the State of Hawaii issued a correction on its emergency alert system. It took nearly half an hour, the governor later confessed, because he could not remember the login for his official Twitter account. The White House issued no communication until later in the day, when a deputy press secretary said in a statement that the president had been briefed on the incident and that "this was purely a state exercise." This may be a lifetime first, but that morning, as I read an AP article quoting North Korea's official communist newspaper, I found myself agreeing with its assessment of the mayhem in Hawaii as a "tragicomedy."

From the safety of my apartment in Oakland, California, I had two colliding thoughts: First, I was glad on that particular Saturday morning to be headed to the farmers' market and not to be still serving as secretary of homeland security. Second, it was clear that the incident, however bizarre it appeared on the surface, revealed problems far more numerous and serious than those being discussed in the media. My what-if brain took over: What if this had been not an accident but a hack by a hostile actor, intended to cause chaos not only in one American city or state but many? What if the goal had been to distract Americans and provide cover for another type of attack? What if a hostile government changed its defensive or offensive posture based on the confusion in Hawaii and that caused the US military to miscalculate in turn, leading to an unintended escalation? What if public panic caused traffic accidents or heart attacks? A breakdown in public order? Runs on banks and airports?

The mishap revealed systemic failures at many levels. There seemed to be no coherent command and control within the government of Hawaii nor clear lines between the state of Hawaii and the federal government. Neither FEMA nor the Federal Communications Commission, which operates federal alert systems, could help in the moment because the error occurred at the state level, and the two systems did not "talk" to each other.

Communication with the public was abysmal. Outdated software meant there was no way to retract the warning as soon as it became clear it was sent in error. It fell to Defense Secretary James Mattis to inform the media that there had been no change in North Korea's defense posture during the confusion. The White House put out a statement saying that the president had been briefed, noting, "This was purely a state exercise." Homeland Security chief Kirstjen Nielsen said the next day the false alarm was "unfortunate" and that authorities are "all working to make sure it doesn't happen again." The first comment from President Trump also came a day later. "I love that they took responsibility, but we're going to get involved," he said of Hawaii's officials. "Their attitude and what they want to do, I think it's terrific. They took responsibility, they made a mistake." Asked how to prevent a similar blunder, Trump said, "Well, we hope it won't happen again, but part of it is that people are on edge, and maybe eventually we'll solve the problem and they won't have to be so on edge."

This is not leadership. A leader communicates clearly about what is known and what is not known, what the problem is and what the plan is for fixing it. That's what people want to know. Americans expect to hear from their president on issues of national security. Of course, it is easy to fob off responsibility on a careless or confused switch operator in Honolulu or on the employee's bosses or to shrug off an embarrassing accident at the state level because the federal government was not involved. That is not leadership either. People were "on edge" because the tensions between the United States and North Korea had reached frightening levels, and the siren incident fit into a narrative of possible military escalation. We do not expect the president to weigh in on every technical glitch or misplaced pallet of Band-Aids in a disaster zone. But we do expect the president to set the tone, to communicate calm and competence. That is true in a real crisis and sometimes even in an imagined crisis, such as the one in Hawaii.

The aftermath of the false alarm was predictable. There were public apologies, lots of them, and investigations galore at the state and the federal level. Those found responsible were either fired, retired, or disciplined—appropriately, in my view. Better oversight by the FCC of the state radio alert system was promised. The US Pacific Command acknowledged it too had erred, by sounding sirens from Joint Base Pearl Harbor, without confirming the validity of the missile alert. In all the personnel churn at the White House, it was revealed that a planned drill at the principal level, meaning new cabinet secretaries and top military and intelligence officials learning what to do in the event of a real missile crisis, had not been able to be scheduled during the first year of the Trump administration. The first year. None of this knowledge is comforting.

But blaming, which is all too common in politics, is different from learning, which is all too rare in government. Of the many troubling aspects of this episode, I am most bothered by the lack of information making its way to the public. If this had been a real alert, how many people would know what to do, where to go, or how to be in touch with their families?

We know in homeland security that there will always be those who seek to undermine our society and outsmart the systems we design to protect it, no matter how evolved those systems are. Technological advances will be unending, and if the past decades are any indication, the private sector is likely to be a hop, skip, and a jump—or in many cases, a light-year—ahead of the public sector. The question is where the advantage will reside: technology has the ability to advance security and at the same time to do great harm.

Other threats to the homeland are intractable too. The poverty and violence that drive migrants from Central America and Mexico north across the US border is not going to magically disappear. Climate change will not reverse itself and unburden FEMA of its heavier load. A solid containment plan for pandemic eludes us still. We will not run short any time soon of lost and troubled young people searching for a combat weapon they can buy over the counter or for a violent cause to join on the internet. Content on social media and the dark web allows individuals to become radicalized online in ways that defy predictive analytics. Sometimes there is an ideology associated with plans for violence—whether racial, political, or religious—and just as often there is not. The threats we face go far beyond the remnants of al-Qaeda, ISIS, or neo-Nazis and other forms of domestic terrorism. And cybersecurity of critical infrastructure will continue to be a major vulnerability for the foreseeable future.

This is not to say that we should surrender to the dangers but rather that we must without regard to ideology or politics divide the threats into those we can control and those we are not yet able to and then come up with effective strategies for managing and reducing each set of risks. Whenever I fly, I note the majority of my fellow passengers madly texting or blithely thumbing through magazines while the flight attendants conduct the federally mandated safety briefing. Yes, we have heard it all before, and yes, it is boring. But should that information be needed, it's going to be too late to put down the phone when it matters. What responsibility are we willing to take for ourselves? The passengers cannot control whether the plane crashes, but they can control whether they are informed and prepared to act correctly in an emergency.

There are things we can do to reduce risk. If we build suburbs in floodplains and wildfire zones and fancy houses on eroding coastlines ever more prone to extreme weather events, it is a poor use of money, effort, and, potentially, the lives of first responders to demand that FEMA and local governments come to the rescue each time when predictable dangers strike. Again, this is not to say FEMA gets a hall pass but rather that we must direct resources where they are most needed and where they can do the most to save lives, alleviate suffering, and improve public safety. When an entire society nears collapse, as we saw in Puerto Rico following Hurricane Maria, the full arsenal of federal government resources must be brought to bear.

There are homeland security responsibilities at the personal, societal, and governmental level, yet it is the government's role people most often hear about, most notably the failures. This is one of the unfortunate realities of homeland security—the false missile alerts and underwear bombers stick in people's minds, while the many, many successes go unknown, unnoticed, or unacknowledged. We do not publicize disasters thwarted. Sometimes the best security is that which is unseen and not talked about in public, such as the work that goes on at the National Targeting Center. Sometimes it happens in plain view but seems banal. The TSA screens up to two million travelers a day, more than any other law-enforcement agency on earth, but it is known more for the inconvenience and indignities inflicted on the public in the process rather than the threats TSA agents deter and intercept. US Border Patrol agents work in brutal physical environments and provide humanitarian assistance as often as they whip out the handcuffs, but they are perpetually maligned by some immigrant advocate groups as if they are a rogue law-enforcement agency. All of these public servants deserve better.

The US Coast Guard, the fifth branch of the US armed forces, delivers more bang for the buck than any other service. With forty-three thousand personnel and a budget that is a tiny fraction of the US Navy's, the Coast Guard, under the direction of the Department of Homeland Security, has one of the largest mission sets in the federal government. It secures the vast international coastlines and the domestic waterways and ports of the United States. It conducts thousands of search and rescue missions each year. It seizes drugs, interdicts undocumented migrants at sea, patrols critical maritime infrastructure (including levees, locks, and energy and freshwater plants), escorts cargo vessels carrying billions of dollars in trade, investigates pollution, and saves wildlife.

Thanks to the efforts of these homeland security professionals and some effective policy decisions over the years, DHS has improved command, control, and coordination among intelligence, law-enforcement, national-security, and emergency agencies considerably. Many of the open seams revealed by the failure to stop the 9/11 attacks have been closed. In its second decade, the Department of Homeland Security is becoming better at identifying where vulnerabilities and threats intersect and how to shut down many of the dangers. The two dozen component agencies thrown together after 9/11 work together more effectively than they did when I became DHS secretary in 2009 and will no doubt work even better under future secretaries. Once we summon political will and common sense, we should be capable of figuring out the mess with congressional oversight of DHS.

That's the good news. Homeland security works when we adhere to proven principles of law enforcement, national security, and disaster management and when we integrate those principles with the best data science and other technological innovations available and update them constantly. We get into trouble when political ideology is thrown into the mix. In a huge and open nation, there will never be enough money, gates, guns, or guards to run down every potential threat. As every prosecutor knows, discretion is key. A stubborn or willful misreading of the threat environment leads to poor management of resources and results in failure. And in this regard, I regret to say, we are backsliding terribly.

Border protection is one such area. We know from early attempts during the Bush administration and from some our own missteps during the Obama years that vetting travelers primarily by country of origin is not a very effective way of catching terrorists. From a law-enforcement perspective, a dragnet approach, such as the ban on travelers from predominantly Muslim countries (the so-called Muslim ban implemented by the Trump administration in early 2017, a later version of which was upheld by the US Supreme Court in 2018), creates unnecessarily large data sets and diverts CPB resources that could be better spent identifying and thwarting actual threats. This is the opposite of "shrinking the haystack," which allows for more precise targeting of traveler data. From a political perspective, such policies antagonize allies in the Islamic world and provide propaganda points to adversaries.

The Muslim ban has led to a general erosion of trust between the United States and partner nations and in particular those on the list. Optically, it has become more difficult for those nations to openly or robustly share threat information with the United States, and where intel sharing gets pushed into the shadows, it necessarily becomes less robust. Similarly, in the other direction, partners become less publicly able to rely upon and accept intel we share with them for both trust and political reasons. They become as a result less reliable partners in endeavoring to mitigate threats to the United States on their soil prior to those threats maturing. This means we become a go-it-alone nation in protecting our own security rather than a cooperative force with partners.

Similarly, the border wall between the United States and Mexico threatens to waste money, attention, and political capital and antagonize Mexico, our neighbor and ally. This too can have security implications down the line. In 2013, Mexican intelligence helped the

United States foil a plot by an Iranian American who tried to recruit a Mexican drug cartel to bomb a Washington restaurant where the Saudi ambassador to the United States dined. We would like Mexico to continue helping us in this way.

The choice is not between an open border and a wall. I am all for border security and the rule of law, as are most Americans. We need to stop wasting time on hysterical arguments over false choices and focus on smart, cost-effective solutions to securing the border. As I have written in previous chapters, there are far more effective measures involving technology and hybrid approaches combining physical barriers, surveillance, and the presence of agents that can secure the border. We must also take a hard look at the continued push for funding additional hires of Border Patrol agents, in light of the agency's thousands of currently unfilled positions. Searching, interviewing, hiring, training, and deploying agents into the field is a process that can take years. Paradoxically, these personnel and training functions use up CBP resources as well.

Immigration enforcement is another area in which we are moving backward. One of the bigger but less publicized shortcomings of our immigration system relates not to border security but to immigration enforcement. The Trump administration proposes hiring an additional 1,000 ICE attorneys and an additional 370 immigration judges to reduce the immigration court backlog and make the removal process more efficient. This is reasonable but, again, must be tied to comprehensive immigration reform.

Even before the mayhem caused by zero tolerance, the often-draconian deportation policies under the Trump administration amount to a misuse of ICE resources and deepen a culture of fear in immigrant communities throughout the United States. Already, many undocumented immigrants will refuse to cooperate with local law enforcement when they are witnesses to—or victims of—a crime. Others do not seek health care (increasing ER costs and undermining preventive care, like vaccines) or dare present themselves to the DMV to obtain a driver's license. None of this advances the security of our communities.

In terms of prioritizing deportations, the threatened reversal and ongoing ambiguity regarding DACA recipients represents another waste. It is a waste of human capital to deport educated taxpayers or students on track to become taxpayers, as well as a waste of limited ICE resources to hunt down and deport law-abiding DACA recipients instead of focusing more resources on criminals and border crime.

Climate change is the ultimate threat and is largely unaddressed by the Trump administration. This is homeland security malpractice and an absolute tragedy. By withdrawing from the Paris Accord in 2017, the United States now finds itself isolated, in the same company as Syria and Nicaragua, the only other countries in the world not to ratify the global agreement to limit global warming to well below 2 degrees Celsius above preindustrial times. As part of the agreement, the Obama administration pledged to reduce domestic greenhouse gas emissions by about 28 percent below 2005 levels by 2025 and commit up to $3 billion in aid for poorer countries by 2020. By May 2017, the United States had delivered $1 billion before it stepped out of the agreement. Homeland security is a matter of reality and of perception. Abdicating American values and leadership undercuts the DHS mission of enhancing security while "protecting the American way of life."

We are left with a false security narrative, security theater run amok. And Americans are left in a state of unbearable anxiety, seeing threats in the wrong places and ignoring others in front of their eyes, because of this false narrative. We have worked for nearly two decades at DHS to help the American people feel empowered as agents of their own security. It is imperative that we do not go back to the time when people feel they are victims of forces beyond their control.

DHS must continue to educate Americans about their responsibilities and the need for awareness at the personal and community level. Even before people call 911, bystanders and neighbors are often first on the scene. This is homeland security at its most basic community level. When I was secretary, we created the "See Something, Say Something" campaign, modeled on the NYPD's program, to empower people and to elevate them from being victims, from being passive to being proactive. We worried when we started the program about prank calls, whether caused by mischief or malice against neighbors or family members. But that is not what happened. Instead, we saw increased public awareness directing us to things like unattended packages and other legitimately suspicious activity.

We have of course also seen heartbreaking failure in this area. The Parkland, Florida, school shooter threw out lots of signals prior to murdering seventeen people at Marjory Stoneman Douglas High School on Valentine's Day in 2018, but they all fell through the cracks. This cannot stop us from being vigilant and trying harder. Again, learn and move forward. We must get beyond the epic system failures that took place at every level before and during the Parkland shooting. In this area, we must also look beyond the nominal limits of "homeland" security. As part of public engagement, I include laying the groundwork for repairing the alliances and partnerships in the post-Trump era that are essential to our homeland security in an ever more dangerous world.

We should help alleviate the conditions in Central America that cause so many to flee to the United States. We should inventory all of our existing intelligence-sharing agreements so that we can identify gaps to fill and areas that need strengthening. We should challenge the community of nations to work collectively, to, for example, establish enforceable standards governing cybersecurity. The United States must reengage and reassert our leadership position in the world. The more we engage and the sooner we do it, the safer we will be.

CHAPTER 12
A Road Map

It was early January 2013, a few days after my father died, and I was at his house in Albuquerque cleaning out his things. I was in a reflective mood. My dad was my rock, and he was gone. I was grateful to have gotten time off over the holidays the previous year to spend with him, my brother, my sister, and their kids. Less than two weeks earlier, knowing it would be his last Christmas, we bundled him up in his wheelchair for our traditional Christmas Eve walk through Albuquerque's Old Town to see the beautiful luminarias. These poignant images also included flashes of our irrepressible family humor. My dad's declining health did not deter my niece Carrie and my nephew David from another family tradition: the annual pranking of Aunt Janet. Unbeknown to me, they removed the head of a toy horse, coated it in fake blood, and somehow managed to sneak it into my bed. Then they rigged up a speaker to blast "It's Beginning to Look a Lot Like Christmas." And so it was that on the morning of December 25, the US secretary of homeland security woke up screaming, and it had nothing to do with the underwear bomber.

I was thinking about all this when my cell phone rang with a White House number. I answered and was surprised to hear not an operator but President Obama. "Hi, Janet," he said. "I'm thinking about you and wanted to check in." He was speaking not as the president of the United States or as my boss but as a decent and caring person, knowing that I was going through a painful life passage. He had a country to run and wars to fight, and I had dishes to pack and clothes to give away, yet we took a few minutes to talk about my dad and what it means to lose a parent. I do not know if other world leaders do this, but I am grateful to have served with one who did.

The new year was shaping up as a time of change in other ways as well. The years of around-the-clock vigilance had taken a toll. I was physically exhausted. I knew what it would take to do the job for the next four years, and I wanted to give the president time to appoint a successor who could serve throughout his second term. I also wanted to organize a transition as supportive and productive as the one my predecessor had afforded me. It was time to start that process. A few months after my dad's death, my longtime executive assistant, Jacquee Wright, who had been with me since I was attorney general, announced she was retiring and moving home to Arizona. Shortly after that, I accepted a position as president of the University of California, resigned from the Department of Homeland Security, and moved to Oakland, where many of my college friends, my brother, and his family live.

It was a good transition at the right time in my life. And it afforded me the perspective to look back on what I have seen during a career in law enforcement, politics, and homeland security and now leading the largest and finest public research university in the country. Americans are problem solvers. We can stem the erosion that has taken place in recent years and put homeland security back on track by implementing some commonsense principles.

I have tried to pull back the curtain and demystify what homeland security is about. It does not have to be scary or seem impossible. It does require problem-solving, ingenuity, and a willingness on the part of every person to get involved. Fortunately, Americans are good at all of this. If I were to leave a note in the desk of the next secretary of homeland security, here is what I would say:

Start each day by assessing the risks we face. Then prioritize them by magnitude, likelihood, and immediacy. Assign science-based evidence a higher value than ideology. You may think undocumented immigrants are a major threat, but the data show climate change affects more lives in more ways. Your next step is to allocate resources—whether that means money, technology, or people—according to the danger each threat poses. You must consistently share the facts that support your reasoning, even if the president and members of Congress don't like them. Push back against those who refute facts and science. No matter what you do, rely on proven law-enforcement methods and enhance these capabilities with the best and most appropriate technologies for the task. Be open to innovation, because technology is always changing. Collaborate, collaborate, and then collaborate some more with our law-enforcement, military, and intelligence agencies at the federal level and with our thousands of partners in state, local, and tribal governments. (Keep in mind that sovereign tribal lands form much of our border with Mexico.) Collaborate with neighbors, allies, and even adversaries with whom we have common interests. Hint: I would have gotten nowhere with my counterparts in the Middle East or Mexico, or anywhere else for that matter, if I started my discussion with "America first!"

Third, communicate relentlessly with the American people and hold them as accountable for homeland security at the personal level as they hold the department at the government level. Do this by informing and empowering, not scolding. Remember, you have 325 million partners out there, and they are waiting to hear from you. Fourth, adhere rigorously to constitutional protections in the performance of the DHS mission. And finally, work to streamline the contraption of congressional oversight so that DHS leaders can spend more time getting their jobs done and less time talking about getting their jobs done.

If you start by prioritizing risks, then you will see that the irreversible threat of climate change emerges as a central element of homeland security. The magnitude is universal, affecting every community in the United States and the world. The threat likelihood is 100 percent, even if we continue to disagree along political lines as to whether human activity is the primary cause. But we must resist the fallacy of mistaking climate change for weather. Climate change is here, so it passes the immediacy test. Corresponding policy changes are needed at the federal, state, and local level as a result. Both the public sector and the private sector must take action. We start by adopting policies to reduce greenhouse gas emissions—applying legislative, regulatory, and economic tools. This will reduce the rate of change but not reverse the damage already done. Next, we should adapt our planning and building codes to mitigate against future risks, as many cities are already doing, steering development from higher-risk to lower-risk areas.

After that, you and your team can enhance resilience in a few ways. First, continue to direct resources to FEMA and its local partners to more efficiently and effectively manage disasters made more frequent by climate change. This requires working even more closely with local communities to ensure they are as prepared as they can be. It means furthering the education of individuals, so they are empowered to know what to do and to be in position to manage for themselves in the first hours following a disaster. The persistent challenge of communications interoperability must be addressed. Then, you must incentivize energy-efficient construction methods in the public and private sectors through tax and other policies. Finally, educate and engage the public so that people are prepared for extreme weather events by having and heeding personal evacuation plans, keeping seventy-two hours' worth of essential supplies on hand, and downloading emergency communication apps on their mobile phones. FEMA introduced these two-way communication tools during my tenure, and they are getting more useful all the time.

Our next major metathreat is cybersecurity. The magnitude is nearly universal, affecting every person using the internet, and it is extremely likely that an individual, business, or government has been or will be affected by a data breach of some significance in any given year. The threat is immediate and metastasizing at increasing rates of speed and severity. In April 2018, the United States and Britain issued an unprecedented joint alert, warning of danger from a Russian cyberintrusion, a duck-and-cover drill for the digital age. The cyberthreat is existential, whether it involves the security of our democratic elections or our critical infrastructure. Here too, you can lead the way to see that policies and behavior change at all levels of government, in the private sector and public sector, and at the personal level, involving digital "hygiene," such as password and network security, internet habits, and social media.

The US Cyber Command will continue to coordinate the security of military networks and to address the military dimensions of cyberthreats. On the civilian side, DHS should assume the central coordinating role for nonmilitary government networks and other public-sector concerns. DHS is the appropriate agency for this role since it has overall responsibility for protecting the nation's critical infrastructure. As with climate change, we must also improve our resilience so that we recover quickly from inevitable attacks and minimize damage.

In addition to a cyber-FEMA, we need to take a step backward (or forward, as the case should be) and examine our entire national approach to cybersecurity. As described earlier, a 9/11-style commission should be formed and charged with evaluating the nation's cyberrisk profile, how government and the private sector should be best organized to mitigate that risk, and what the rules of engagement are when a foreign power attacks our cybernetworks.

Applying the principles of magnitude, likelihood, and immediacy, the next homeland security priority is what I will call Terror 3.0, detecting and preventing mass casualty events of all sorts. In terms of casualties, the magnitude and likelihood of mass shootings, trucks as weapons, and other such attacks is relatively low; the number of victims comes nowhere near the number of Americans who die in automobile accidents, for example. But the psychological and societal impact of mass casualty events is immense, pervasive, and ever more troubling. For that reason, it ranks high on the list. As secretary of homeland security, you should put our nation's public health specialists and social scientists to work. Don't wait for the next tragedy to take action. We need better predictors and better intervention strategies. And yes, we must adopt some commonsense gun safety measures to reduce the mayhem. Age limits, background checks, and limits on the type of firepower available for purchase are constitutional and widely popular, demonstrating that, on this topic, the American people are ahead of their elected leaders.

You must help correct the false narrative that the biggest threat to Americans' security is to be found at the southern border. Instead, we need a border that is secured in the right way, with manpower, technology, and air cover that is flexible and adaptable to conditions on the border. Investing billions in a single fixed structure like a wall is a simple invitation to ladders and tunnels. We need a border that is as secure as it can be but one that recognizes its importance as an economic artery, allowing thousands of people and millions of dollars of cargo to cross every day without needless delay. You must work with Mexico to have a twenty-first-century border. In this endeavor they are our partner, not our adversary. Treat them with dignity and decency, as respected neighbors.

In a world of limited resources, you need to make policy based on risk, not fear. That means we redirect our resources from workplace raids designed to scare low-wage workers and instead use them to audit the suspected employers of undocumented workers. This allows us to inflict penalties in a way that will cut down on tax evasion and labor safety violations at the same time, delivering more bang for the law-enforcement buck. You should not send our agents, with their limited time, after well-educated and productive young people brought to the United States illegally as children. You should not instruct ICE agents to put at the top of their arrest list the small-business owners and taxpayers who create jobs and are otherwise law abiding, save for their immigration status.

You need the discipline to leave the low-hanging fruit, the made-for-TV drama of feds in their blue windbreakers hustling away "illegals" in shackles, and to direct our efforts instead to finding and deporting those convicted of serious crimes. The end result is a greater overall impact on public safety. You should cut down on the theatrics for the television cameras and the congressional testimony and White House press conferences, because we know our immigration courts are so hopelessly overloaded that fewer than half of apprehensions result in a deportation order. Instead of satisfying members of Congress with high apprehension rates, it is incumbent on you to point them to the more challenging truth: funds are better spent on immigration courts, where the truly dangerous can be swiftly deported.

Nor does it advance US security to insist blindly on zero tolerance, whatever the cost. In 2017, ICE stationed four agents outside the hospital room of a disabled ten-year-old girl taken across the border for emergency surgery in Corpus Christi, Texas, because the child was undocumented. As soon as she recovered, the child and an adult relative were taken back across the border to Mexico. In another case, US Border Patrol agents detained a nineteen-year-old French citizen who accidentally crossed from British Columbia into Washington State when she was out jogging near an unmarked section of the US-Canadian border. She remained in US custody for two weeks, until she was able to document her citizenship and get released. Not only does it make us look as though US agents are taking a page from the Kim Jong-un handbook of border security, it is an irrational and unacceptable waste of taxpayer dollars and the time of our agents to conduct such nonsensical enforcement. Keep in mind that for each hour one of our agents spends guarding a bedridden child or cap-turing a lost jogger, they have one hour less to intercept a narcotics shipment or catch a criminal. This is an embarrassing way to run a huge country.

Since its inception, the department has been shifting to a model of homeland security based increasingly on risk. By the end of the Obama administration, the percentage of those deported who have been convicted of serious crimes had increased sharply—over 90 percent in 2016 compared to 51 percent in 2009. Enforcement pri-orities must be set according to the threat posed to public safety, not because it looks tough on TV, impresses the boss, or makes for a great election slogan. Don't fall into this trap.

You must also consider our message to the world. Images of incon-solable children and public scoldings from allies and religious leaders stain us as a nation. They hollow our human rights lectures to the rest of the world. They erode our moral authority in other ways too. We cannot call on other countries to "do their share" in defense when we do not do our share in stemming the global refugee crisis, which is now the worst in human history. While the United States has tradi-tionally been the world leader in accepting refugees for resettlement, that leadership has been undercut by the Trump administration. In 2016, the United States accepted 84,994 refugees for resettlement. In his first year in office, President Trump limited that number to 50,000. Canada, with a tenth of our population, accepted the same number in that time frame. Germany, with about a quarter of the US population (around 80 million), is the world leader in refugee resettlement. In 2016, it took in over 700,000 refugees, nearly ten times the US total. It does not reflect American values or engender goodwill and, as a result, enhance US national interests to accept fewer refugee than, for instance, Uganda, which welcomed 489,000 refugees in 2016. On a per capita basis this is some fifty times that of the United States. Stand up for American values when you talk to the president, testify before Congress, and travel abroad.

Next, it is time, after nearly two decades of progress, to revisit the unresolved tensions between privacy and security during the post-9/11 era. Help Americans understand that we have to move beyond the outdated notion that one is achieved at the expense of the other and embrace privacy by design.

You also need to assess carefully the collection of so much metadata, made possible by advances in technology. We have to ask before we gather: What useful intelligence will it actually reveal? We do not want to move away from shrinking the haystack, just because it is relatively easy to capture big data. Adopting a privacy by design strategy throughout government, including within the NSA, if done properly, could both increase the effectiveness of the intel gathering and ensure that people's privacy interests are not being unnecessarily sacrificed. We must design all information collection to enlarge the likelihood of actually detecting plots, conspiracies, or other criminal behavior while at the same time recognizing that the vast majority of human behavior is benign and entitled to privacy from government inspection. That is why integrating privacy by design at the outset adheres both to good security policy and the norms people expect, based on the Constitution.

I have seen privacy and security concerns throughout a long career, as a governor, as state attorney general, as secretary of homeland security, and now, as president of the nation's largest public research university. Since my time as US Attorney, what I have learned is that protecting one's privacy is increasingly difficult because of the rapid growth in the ways in which information is collected and the technological advances that have made data collection, retention, and analysis so much more readily available, whether by the government or by the private sector.

Under the Fourth Amendment, people's reasonable expectations of privacy are given protection from government search and seizure. That is why the concept of privacy by design has such power behind it and why it deserves broader adoption throughout the federal government. I have seen much over the decades, through various roles and technological innovations, as institutions and people struggle with privacy protections in the era of increasingly big data. The problem with data collection is that it is at once too much and too little. On the one hand, the US government tracks 380 million border crossings, 1.8 million airport screenings a day, and one billion data packets a day at the National Targeting Center. That is on the civilian side alone. Do not ever stop asking the question, what among that data is truly useful for security purposes, and what is simply noise that clutters the system?

The trick is to integrate only what is needed when designing any data collection program. In the security world, the assumption is that more is always better. The uproar over Facebook's sale of personal information to Cambridge Analytica reveals that a great many are disturbed by the seemingly endless infringement on information they presume to be private. And just as there should be reasonable limits placed on the government, Congress should address limits on the great information collectors and aggregators in the private sector.

The hosts of these giant social networking platforms have a lot to do to ensure users that their personal information is not being shared without their consent. So, too, the government must be more mindful of the privacy implications of its data collection, even when it is for legitimate national-security and law-enforcement purposes. There are no easy answers here, but greater public awareness of the types of personal information that are collected and shared or sold could lead to needed reforms.

As president of the nation's premier public research university, one with worldwide impact, my perspective has shifted to a degree. At the university, the emphasis on academic freedom and scholarly independence renders some deeply suspicious of any university policy designed to collect information on their whereabouts when they travel internationally. An example: university insurance policy requires us to know where students are, track impending risks, warn students, and be prepared to provide assistance or evacuate in event of danger. We have academics who travel all over the world to conduct research and participate in conferences and the like, and they are covered by the same university insurance, yet some faculty members say they do not want to be tracked. So we have left it to individual departments; many of them resolve the question of risk by deciding that if the scholar wants the university to cover cost of travel, they must comply with the policy of reporting their whereabouts. Designing the right kinds of incentives can encourage the right kinds of behavior.

There are commonsense approaches to some of these issues. Does a policy truly advance our homeland security? Does it do it in the most effective and efficient way possible? Does it do it in a way consistent with the Constitution? Is it forward-thinking enough? Is it proactive and not merely reactive? Is it affordable? These are the questions you must constantly ask.

Homeland security is not only the job of the secretary or of the 240,000 professionals who work for the department; it is everyone's responsibility. The world is dangerous, and we are vulnerable. But we are not helpless or fatalistic, and that is the key difference. I live now in the San Francisco Bay Area, where the smoke from ever deadlier wildfires is so awful that people around me are wearing face masks. It is up to residents to clear defensible spaces around their homes to assist firefighters, but it is incumbent on policy makers to help make communities safer in the broader sense as the impacts of climate change become more severe. It is up to all of us to be aware when we travel, when we go online, and when we go about our daily lives in our communities of circumstances that don't seem right. I'm not talking about whipping out a phone to video and shame perceived rule breakers but to report to authorities such problems as unattended bags or a troubled person assembling an arsenal. And it is up to us to elect leaders who are competent in recognizing and communicating about threats in ways that empower rather than panic the public and who come up with policies to reduce risks while preserving American values. This is not as hard as it sounds, but it does require a willingness to act.

There are big challenges ahead and some significant dangers that we must confront to protect our homeland security in this century. But these challenges are not beyond us. I watched as the United States stood itself back up after 9/11. We are resilient and resourceful. We should have no doubt in ourselves, and neither should our adversaries doubt our capabilities to build a safe, secure, and resilient place, where the American way of life can thrive. If we work together, if we remain vigilant, and if we refuse to live in fear, we can and we will protect our country. We will leave a safer, more resilient country for the next generation to enjoy.

ACKNOWLEDGMENTS

I have many people to thank for their guidance and assistance on what for me was an unfamiliar venture into the world of book writing. Colleen Lawrie and Peter Osnos at PublicAffairs / Hachette Book Group have been incredibly helpful editors, shepherding the book from conception to publication, along with my agent, Peter Bernstein. Karen Breslau, my coauthor, was an ideal collaborator. Her insights and perspective brought much to the final product. Pearly Tan was a resourceful and speedy researcher. Many of my former colleagues at the Department of Homeland Security provided valuable expertise, comments, and historical material. I greatly appreciate the contributions of Rand Beers, Alan Bersin, Mary Ellen Callahan, John Cohen, Caitlin Durkovich, Craig Fugate, Alice Hill, Noah Kroloff, and Amy Shlossman. I also want to thank the former administration and DHS professionals who shared their time for this project: Michael Chertoff, Kathleen Sebelius, Cecilia Muñoz, David Aguilar, Heidi Avery, Paul Benda, Rafael Borrás, Chris Cummiskey, Brian de Vallance, Ryan Gillis, Phil McNamara, Peter Orszag, John Sandweg, Sean Smith, and Mark Sullivan.

My deepest gratitude goes to all the men and women of the Department of Homeland Security who labor day in and day out, often under difficult circumstances, to keep us safe. Their dedication, expertise, and commitment to public service deserve our support and our respect. I cannot thank them enough.

Janet Napolitano

NOTE ON SOURCES

The attacks of September 11, 2001, were the most widely witnessed crime in human history. In the nearly twenty years since those attacks, the US government has developed an enormous homeland security apparatus to prevent anything like it from happening again. Much of that apparatus is unseen by the public, but large parts of it are, by design, very visible to all who live in and visit the United States. Our challenge was to show readers what progress has been achieved since the Department of Homeland Security was created and where key gaps remain, without contributing to a how-to manual for anyone who would do the United States harm.

In reporting this book, we relied on the author's personal experiences as US secretary of homeland security, along with interviews of more than two dozen contemporaries able to verify and deepen these observations. We also relied on the Final Report of the National Commission on Terrorist Attacks Upon the United States (the 9/11 Report); media accounts of the events in question; travel records; public source documents, including the *Congressional Record*; and numerous government reports and speeches by public officials. We were also aided by accounts published by former DHS secretary Tom Ridge, *The Test of Our Times*, and former DHS secretary Michael Chertoff, *Homeland Security: Assessing the First Five Years*, as well as *Playing to the Edge*, by General Michael V. Hayden. We gained additional insight from the works of other authors, including *The United States of Jihad*, by Peter Bergen; *Confront and Conceal*, by David E. Sanger;

Kill or Capture, by Daniel Klaidman; *The Line Becomes a River,* by Francisco Cantú; and *Russian Roulette,* by Michael Isikoff and David Corn. We are indebted to these officials, authors, and journalists for sharing their knowledge.

Any errors are those of the authors.

INDEX

Janet Napolitano is a distinguished public servant with a record of leading large, complex organizations at the federal and state levels. She served as secretary of homeland security from 2009 to 2013. Before that, she was the governor of Arizona, previously serving as attorney general of Arizona and before that as US Attorney for the District of Arizona. She was the first woman to chair the National Governors Association and was named one of the nation's top five governors by *Time* magazine. Since 2013, she has served as the president of the University of California.

PublicAffairs is a publishing house founded in 1997. It is a tribute to the standards, values, and flair of three persons who have served as mentors to countless reporters, writers, editors, and book people of all kinds, including me.

I. F. STONE, proprietor of *I. F. Stone's Weekly*, combined a commitment to the First Amendment with entrepreneurial zeal and reporting skill and became one of the great independent journalists in American history. At the age of eighty, Izzy published *The Trial of Socrates*, which was a national bestseller. He wrote the book after he taught himself ancient Greek.

BENJAMIN C. BRADLEE was for nearly thirty years the charismatic editorial leader of *The Washington Post*. It was Ben who gave the *Post* the range and courage to pursue such historic issues as Watergate. He supported his reporters with a tenacity that made them fearless and it is no accident that so many became authors of influential, best-selling books.

ROBERT L. BERNSTEIN, the chief executive of Random House for more than a quarter century, guided one of the nation's premier publishing houses. Bob was personally responsible for many books of political dissent and argument that challenged tyranny around the globe. He is also the founder and longtime chair of Human Rights Watch, one of the most respected human rights organizations in the world.

· · ·

For fifty years, the banner of Public Affairs Press was carried by its owner Morris B. Schnapper, who published Gandhi, Nasser, Toynbee, Truman, and about 1,500 other authors. In 1983, Schnapper was described by *The Washington Post* as "a redoubtable gadfly." His legacy will endure in the books to come.

Peter Osnos, *Founder*